1

DEAR FATHER

DEAR FATHER

A Message of Love to Priests

by
Catherine de Hueck Doherty

ALBA · HOUSE   NEW · YORK

SOCIETY OF ST. PAUL, 2187 VICTORY BLVD., STATEN ISLAND, NEW YORK 10314

Library of Congress Cataloging in Publication Data

Doherty, Catherine de Hueck, 1900-
    Dear Father: a message of love to priests.

    1. Catholic Church—Clergy. I. Title.
BX1912.D54   253   78-31389
ISBN 0-8189-0377-5

Imprimatur:
† J.R. Windle
Bishop of Pembroke
March 1, 1978

Produced in the United States of
America by the Fathers and Brothers of the
Society of St. Paul, 2187 Victory Boulevard,
Staten Island, New York, 10314, as part of their
communications apostolate.

3 4 5 6 7 8 9 (Current Printing: first digit).

MY APPRECIATION

Anyone who knows Catherine Doherty would expect her to treat this subject just as she has done, frankly, directly, simply, lovingly. She portrays an exalted and innate idea of the Priesthood which characterizes any references she ever makes to it in all her writings. "Priest," she seems to say, "you are God-with-us, chosen by him to guide, and show us how to love him and how to love one another. Why should you be restless, dissatisfied, angry? Why look to other pastures? You have everything. Be what you are supposed to be—our friend, teacher, healer, servant. Be what Jesus wants you to be—another himself. Then your worries about identity will fade; you will find satisfaction and happiness; then you will no longer want to be other than you are; then you will be a bearer of peace and of hope to many confused people seeking guidance in today's doubt-filled world."

This message, the author presents, in an atmosphere of a profound love for priests which can only flow from a love for the Eternal Priest and his chosen ones that has grown over the years through prayer and penance. Her thrust is to encourage, to inspire, to protect, and to activate the priest as Christ's ambassador of love to all members of his flock, but especially to those who are yearning for their Lord.

†J. R. Windle
Bishop of Pembroke
March 1, 1978

CONTENTS

Introduction

Many years ago, Catherine's husband Eddie received a letter in which he was asked: "What *is* a priest?" He told me that he puzzled over the question for some time and then went to see Catherine who was seated at her desk typing. "Someone has asked me," he said, "what a priest is. Do you know?" He said that she, without saying a word, picked up a pencil and wrote hastily on a piece of scrap-paper the following:

A priest is a lover of God,
  a priest is a lover of men,
  a priest is a holy man
  because he walks before the face of the All-Holy.

A priest understands all things,
  a priest forgives all things,
  a priest encompasses all things.

The heart of a priest is pierced, like Christ's,
  with the lance of love.

The heart of a priest is open, like Christ's,
  for the whole world to walk through.

The heart of a priest is a vessel of compassion,
  the heart of a priest is a chalice of love,
  the heart of a priest is the trysting place
  of human and divine love.

A priest is a man whose goal is to be another Christ;
a priest is a man who lives to serve.

A priest is a man who has crucified himself
so that he too may be lifted up
and draw all things to Christ.

A priest is a man in love with God.

A priest is the gift of God to man
and of man to God.

A priest is the symbol of the Word made flesh,
a priest is the naked sword of God's justice,
a priest is the hand of God's mercy,
a priest is the reflection of God's love.

Nothing can be greater in this world than a priest,
nothing but God himself.

This remarkable poem, etched in wood, is printed on the chapel wall of Vianney House, a dormitory for visiting priests located at Madonna House in Combermere, Ontario, Canada. The poem has been printed in leaflet form, and many times reprinted, so great is the demand for it.

The poem came out of the heart of Catherine Doherty as has this book, *Dear Father*, addressed to the priests of the world. The book, like the poem, springs from an awesome love for priests and a clear, deep, vivid insight into that mystery of faith by which those who really believe *know* that a priest is *another Christ*.

This poem and this book are lovely gifts from Catherine's heart to the priests and people of the Church but they are, in a sense, only by-products of a far more wonderful gift—a radically new type of Christian community (she prefers the word "family") composed of laymen, laywomen and priests: the Madonna House Apostolate. Over the years Catherine has insisted that our Lady is the real foundress and that she,

Catherine, is only a "proxy" for our Lady. The Madonna House headquarters is also a Marian shrine, approved by the Church under the title of Our Lady of Combermere. The total membership at present is approximately 130—90 women and 40 men. 14 of the men are priests, including one bishop. 51 other priests have made a commitment to the Madonna House way of life through an associate membership, remaining under the jurisdiction of their respective bishops. At present there are 15 mission houses.

What is it that binds the men, women and priests of Madonna House together? It is a common commitment to create a community of love in Christ and to express this love in the works of the Apostolate. Catherine sees us as "pilgrims in this world proclaiming the second coming of Christ when all things will be restored to him." Like all Christian pilgrims the members travel in poverty to find security only in Christ; journey in chastity to serve and love Christ in men; live in obedience to be concerned only with the will of God. The work of the Apostolate is to restore man and his institutions to Jesus Christ by fulfilling the immense law of his love and truly incarnating the Gospel in the daily life of its members.

The heart and core of the Madonna House way of life has come to us in the form of certain words which Catherine heard in her heart in the late twenties when God was calling her to establish this Apostolate. They contain the very essence of the Gospel of Jesus Christ and are so concise that they are printed on a small card and known to us now as the "Little Mandate." Since the Little Mandate is the heart of the Gospel, it has been given by God to Catherine not only for Madonna House but for the whole Church, indeed for the whole world:

> *Arise—go! Sell all you possess . . . give it directly,*
> *personally to the poor. Take up my cross (their cross)*
> *and follow me—going to the poor—being poor—being*
> *one with them—one with me.*

> *Little—be always little . . . simple—poor—childlike.*

*Preach the Gospel with your life—without compromise—
listen to the Spirit—he will lead you.*

Do little things exceedingly well for love of me.

Love—love—love, never counting the cost.

*Go into the market place and stay with me ... pray ... fast
. . . pray always . . . fast.*

*Be hidden—be a light to your neighbor's feet. Go without
fears into the depth of men's hearts . . . I shall be with
you.*

Pray always. I will be your rest.

Catherine has given many talks to the Madonna House
priests, to our associate priests, to the many hundreds of priests
who have come here and to those to whom she speaks all over
the continent. Her message to us is very simple: "Teach the
Little Mandate by incarnating it in your own life." She insists
that there is only one way to teach—by example.

The Lord called me from the Basilian Fathers into the
Madonna House Apostolate 25 years ago and I am now
completing my forty-second year of priesthood. I had been
with the Basilians for 32 years as student, novice, seminarian
and priest, almost totally immersed in academics at the
university and graduate levels, accustomed to a rather
comfortable life-style in Catholic institutions from age nine. So
for me the plunge into the Little Mandate was turbulent and
traumatic, but indeed a treasure hidden in the wilderness. For
25 years my heart has overflowed in praise and gratitude to the
Lord Jesus and His mother who, together called me into this
new and amazing priestly vocation.

The members of Madonna House wear a silver cross as a
sign of their committment: on the cross are engraved two
words, *Pax* and *Caritas* (Peace and Love). I was one of the first

Madonna House priests to receive the cross. The Director of Priests, Father John Callahan, bestowed it with the simple words *Accipe Crucem* (Receive the cross) to which each priest replied *Deo Gratias* (Thanks be to God). It was one of the most glorious and thrilling moments of my life. It was a holy moment, an awesome moment and, it seems, a moment of light and of fire. I tried to capture a flash of that light, a spark of that fire, in these words that came rising like a melody out of my heart:

Accipe Crucem!

Two words were spoken
And the darkness of my soul
Was broken
By a flash of light
So bright
That I was blinded
Momentarily
And could not seem to see
The father of our priests
Or what it was
That he held out to me.

Accipe crucem!

Two words entwined!
Two logs that bind
Themselves together!
One is straight and tall
And reaches to the sky;
The other stretches wide to fall
Across the dim horizon
Of the days and years
That have been given me
In this new family.

Accipe crucem!

Take up the Cross
And follow me.
Be not afraid,
For it is I, the Lord,
Who speak to thee.
The words are mine:
You do but hear the echo of them
Rising from the hills of Palestine
To come to rest this day
In priestly hearts of clay
That I have formed and breathed upon
And wed
To the heart of her
Who gave my heart to me.
The Mother of Divinity.

Accipe Crucem!

Take it! Wear it!
It is my mother's cross
That I have willed to be
The sign I give
For all the world to see
That you are born, like me,
Of her Maternity.
It is the seal engraved
Forever on your hearts
Of my own love for her,
Of hers for me—
A flaming love
Of such intensity
That it embraced humanity
And led us both to Calvary.

Accipe Crucem!

Take the Cross
And lift it high;
Climb upon it,
As did I.
Be another me,
My brothers,
And let this cross the symbol be
That my priests and laity
Are one in apostolic love
As she was one with me
From Bethlehem to Calvary.

Accipe Crucem!

"Take up the Cross!
It is the only way
To love,
The only way
To peace,
The only way
To joy,
The only way
To me
Who am
Eternally
The only source
Of all Delight
And Ecstacy."

Through the Virgin Mary, and by a special gift of the Holy Spirit, hundreds of priests are being specially chosen by the Lord and drawn into a new type of brotherhood of priests, brothers of the Lord in a true and real sense, sharing his own intimacy with his Father and his Mother, brothers of a new order, born in a new day, carriers of light in the darkness, atoners. Our hands and all of us are chalices that will hold the new wine. We are breads that will be eaten up as food for the new saints. We are the beginning of an endless and immense family that weds soul to soul. We are called to lead and spearhead the Lord's pebbles, the little ones. We are given his own power to destroy his enemy, and we will destroy him.

I pray that every priest who reads this book will be given the gift of understanding and penetrate into its heights and depths. The Lord is asking of us, my brothers, *to remember who we are*. He wants us to give him poverty and obedience. He wants us to give him all of ourselves so he can fashion of us torches of light that will illuminate the darkness of the kingdom of his loved ones who are perishing from hunger and for whom we have been ordained.

The Lord speaks powerfully to every priest through Catherine's book, *Dear Father*, because she has not only prayed for priests from her youth but has offered her life for them. The priests of Madonna House want to pass on to you, our brother-priests, what the Lord has spoken to us through Catherine. We want to do it by living out the Little Mandate, the Gospel without compromise, according to the guidelines the Lord has given us:

A prophetic word of Catherine to the priests of Madonna House

The priests of the Apostolate
shall not fear;
shall put all their trust in Me;
shall go to My Mother
in the dark of the night
which may be their day;
shall be on the battlefields
of the world;
shall not wait for the world
to come to them: they will
go to the world;
shall be eaten up and I will

replenish them even as I did
the twelve loaves of bread;
shall be humble, and through My Mother
I will grant them simplicity of heart;
shall be childlike, and I will make
them towers of strength;
shall be poor: then I shall give them
wealth untold to feed My poor;
shall unceasingly pray for growth in faith:
then I shall give them the faith of martyrs;
shall teach by example—Me: then I shall
reveal Myself through them to all
they will meet;
shall not be concerned as to what to do,
when and how: I will speak to them
in the duty of the moment, the need of
the apostolate and the hunger of souls;
shall love, cherish and protect My Bride,
the Church, and then she will nurse them
at her breasts that are sweeter than wine;
shall be men of prayer: I have prayed always;
shall be in the desert: they will find Me there;
shall seek knowledge of the things of My Father,
Mine and the Holy Spirit. My Mother will
guide them in the seeking;
shall be men of peace, for I will give them
My peace;
will scorn human respect, for I am the
Lord, their God;
will preach, live and do little things
well for the love of Me, for I need the
world to see the secret of
immensity, infinity, sanctity
in little things done well
for love of Me;
will not be afraid to take up the cords of justice
and show the face of My anger to their confreres:
for the wounds these inflict on Me are deep;

will take a staff, but no purse,
  and go forth as did the ones that walked with Me;
shall bless all peoples and all things on their way,
  and I will give their blessing the strength of Mine:
  the world needs My blessing;
shall be men of caritas *and of* pax, *and if they are*
  I shall be their Novice Master to the end of time.

Rev. Gene Cullinane
Madonna House
Combermere, Ont.
July, 1978

CHAPTER ONE

DON'T DESERT US!

In the past I have written books entitled *Dear Bishop, Dear Seminarian,* and *Dear Sister.* I love bishops, seminarians and religious but not exactly in the same way that I love you, God's priests who are charged with the daily spiritual care of God's people. It is because of my special love for you that I have waited so long to put down in book form my feelings for you. My love for you and respect for your special ministry has deepened and grown throughout my life.

Long ago, when I was about eleven or twelve, and far away in a convent of the Sisters of Sion in Ramleh near Alexandria, Egypt, a Jesuit priest gave us little ones a talk. He was holy and simple. He touched my young heart deeply. However, I didn't like it when he asked us to "pray for priests when we became a little more grown up." I asked myself, "Why should I wait an eternity—until I reach eighteen or nineteen—to pray for priests?" I spoke privately with the priest and explained my longing to pray for priests at once.

The Jesuit looked intently and earnestly at me and asked if I truly desired to pray for priests. When I responded affirmatively, he placed his hand upon my head, prayed to the Trinity, patted my cheek and said, "Now, I have blessed you so that, as young as you are, you can pray for priests. Don't forget to do so, child!"

I have never forgotten that special blessing. Even as a child, I loved priests with my whole heart. In my youthful mind, I firmly believed that Christ left us priests because he didn't want to leave us orphans or to part from us. I didn't understand a great deal about the Mystical Body and the many ways Christ remains in our midst. However, I sensed the very special role that priests played in Christ's plan and I found it terribly important to pray for them.

Since the age of twelve, therefore, I have continued to pray for priests. Except for the period when I with my family, was fleeing the communist revolution and I was too sick and weak to pray (weighing barely eighty-two pounds), I have acted upon the blessing given to me in Egypt so many decades ago.

I have stored up many things in my heart and many feelings which for so long I was hesitant or afraid to express. Before Vatican II, there were many sentiments and thoughts that one simply wouldn't think of expressing. Now, however, at the age of seventy-seven, I am not afraid, as I was in my youth, to face you, my priests, and share with you my heart.

I have actually written this book a thousand times over in my mind and heart. Yet, even now as I attempt to write it out I doubt that I will be able to convey to you my love for the priesthood and for each one of you priests of God.

Though it is difficult to write about my personal love for you, I must try. It is important for us the laity to communicate to you, dear Fathers, both our feelings and our needs. In this book, which I visualize as letters written to you, I will convey to you the need we laity have of being guided by our shepherds. We long to hear your voices echoing the call of the one shepherd you represent so tangibly for us. If we do not hear his voice through you, how shall we hear it? Lately, your reassuring voices have either been muted or simply drowned out by the din of a noisy and confused world. We need to hear your voices clearly and we need to hear them now. Our pastures once so green and nourishing for us are being scorched by the searing heat of materialism, selfishness, and doubt. Only your voices united with the voice of the Good Shepherd can lead us to verdant fields once again. The Prince of Darkness is clouding minds, frightening the flock, forcing us to huddle together, uncertain of the direction we must travel in.

But in the present twilight, we the laity are confident that in the face of danger, dear Fathers, you will stand by us and lead us.

At Madonna House, we insist on addressing priests as "Father." Though some prefer to be called simply by their first name we find it impossible to comply with their wish. We recognize too clearly the fact that the priest provides for his spiritual family as surely as a father for his natural family. A natural father is the "bread winner." A priest is a "bread giver" in the Eucharist. As we begin to learn something about God the Father's love for us through experiencing our own father's love for our own family, we learn even more about God's paternal love through your own love of all families. Thus we call you, "Father."

A father is a man who has begotten children. He has a family he must look after. He must provide for the necessities of food, shelter, clothing, education and medical care. He must be present to his family and give them all his love, care and attention. A father is the head of a community of love. Together with his wife, he forms an atmosphere of love conducive not only to healthy human growth but to spiritual growth as well. By example, a father preaches his loudest sermons and teaches his greatest lessons. It is from his own tender, responsible actions that his children learn the heart and the art of loving. Though loving his own family above all others, a father is also aware of the needs of his neighbors as well. In fact, according to his state in life and concrete situation, a father is concerned with the needs of the whole world. In all cases, however, a truly loving father is willing to submit his own needs to those of others. This is the ideal we the laity have of fathers.

We call you "Father" because you begot us in the mystery of a tremendous love affair between you and God. Because you participate in the one priesthood of Christ. You are wedded to the Church, his bride. Even should the law of celibacy be rescinded, you will still be wedded to the Church, and it still will have to take precedence over everything in your life.

We call you "Father" and we are your "family." We need

you desperately. We need you where God has placed you, at the head of our family, just as he has placed human fathers in the midst of their families to nurture and love them.

Whenever an ordinary, human father abandons his family to fulfill his own immediate needs, he creates a truly tragic situation. His entire family, especially his children, are left confused, frightened and lost. The fact that so many human fathers have abandoned their duties accounts for so much of the anarchy that has befallen the world. The large number of priests who have abandoned their duties accounts for a great deal of the pain in the Church throughout the world.

Why so many priests have abandoned their spiritual families is difficult to say. Perhaps, under the pressures of changing values, they suddenly placed their "own needs" before the needs of their family. I would never judge harshly the decision of any priest because I know the pressures and burdens priests bear and the spiritual agonies they encounter. However, remember, dear Fathers, you are not alone. Christ is with you. We, your children, need you.

I would like to suggest, dear Fathers, that you meditate often on the state and plight of the laity you serve. We are young, middle-aged, or elderly. Some of us are married, some single. We are both well educated and illiterate. We are rich and poor. However, all of us are like the grass, here today and gone tomorrow. Nevertheless, you can learn from us. Consider for a moment the situation of the father of a family. He works hard for his family to fulfill their needs. At times he dreams of greener fields opening up to him. However, if he loves his family he will not follow those dreams if they conflict with the real needs of his loved ones. As monotonous, unsatisfying and painful as this may be, loving fathers demonstrate their responsiveness to the needs of others by sticking to the task at hand. Yet, in spite of the two thousand problems that assail the family, things work out. They work out because of love and because of God.

We, the laity, call you by the awesome name "Father," because we see you attending to our spiritual needs. Always keep in mind that you were ordained to serve us, to feed us with the Eucharist, to heal us with anointing, to reconcile us to God and one another in penance, to witness our unions of love in marriage, to preach God's word.

We, the laity, can be healers in many fashions. We the laity can be charismatic healers, doctors, psychologists, psychiatrists and social workers. We can even be counsellors to you our priests! However, we cannot heal in the same sacramental sense that you our priests can heal. If you carry on your own proper healing ministry, you will inspire us the laity to carry God's saving word into the inner city and the suburbs, to the rich and the poor. We can do all this as long as you preach the Gospel to us and nurture us with the sacraments. We need you present to us wherever you may be assigned. We need to be taught by your patience, your kindness, your understanding and your fortitude, what it is to be a Christian.

Have mercy on us, your ordinary, monotonous, dumpy, unleaven flock! Teach us how to love. Teach us how to pray. Inflame our hearts with the desire to wash the feet of our poor brethren, to feed them love, and to preach the Gospel with our lives. Send us forth into the world everywhere—the world of poverty, hunger, misery—so that we may change it because we heard your voice "sending us there"—the Shepherd's voice. Come with us if God appoints you to do so. Lead us, wherever he tells you. But do not desert us in order to fulfill personal ambition or your own immediate needs. Always seek to do God's will and you will fulfill your deepest needs and longings.

The endless pursuit of new life styles or academic degrees and recognition is not the way to priestly happiness. If you follow the voice of the Shepherd and pursue his values you will find peace. True, there will be turmoil in your life, just as there was turmoil in the life of every prophet and in the life of the Divine Master himself. Nevertheless, there will be that unshakeable tranquility that comes from knowing that you are doing God's will and not your own.

The prophets of old were seized with the desire to preach God's word, to teach his people. They emptied themselves for the sake of the people. They spent themselves in God's service meeting the *needs of others*. They gave up secular pursuits to dedicate themselves to the ministry of the word. Be careful, dear Fathers, not to abandon your priestly duties for worldly interests. Never be so taken up with the material aspects of your life (taking care of Church property, raising funds *etc.*) that you neglect your spiritual duties. Never be so anamored with lay life styles as to abandon your priesthood altogether!

You may want to do many noble deeds and accomplish many tasks. You might like to become a psychologist or a foreign missionary. But the most important question to be answered is not what *you* may want, but what *God* wants for you. If you want to become a psychologist or a foreign missionary to fulfill your *own needs* and not to serve others or to do the will of God, you will not be satisfied either as a priest or a person. Love is always the answer and scripture tells us that love is patient, is kind, is gentle. Love seeks to serve others and not the self.

I would like to tell you clearly, dear Father, that any overpowering urge to fulfill your own needs at the expense of the needs of your flock, your spiritual family, does not come from God. The sense of urgency and immediacy to change everything at once to suit your own tastes or inclinations does not spring from the eternally patient, all loving God.

The impatience to fulfill yourself and your desires can only spring from our fallen nature or the Prince of False Promises. Perhaps, in a scientific age it seems foolish to consider the Prince of Darkness. But as I nightly pray and agonize over the problems that beset you, the priests I love so dearly, I hear, figuratively speaking, the barely audible, slithering movements of a serpent. The sound of that slithering serpent will be with us until the end of time. As long as we desire to do our own will rather than God's, that sound will haunt us. To hear that sound is frightening. However, to see some of God's priests apparently following that sound with its promises that are so shallow, is even more frightening. Only the path of prayer can help us in this situation or any like it. When you bow your head in prayer and ask the Lord for guidance, dear Father, realize that you are not praying alone but countless people who rely on you are praying with and for you also.

Have you pondered the Book of Numbers? I was reading it recently. There is in it the question of the census of the tribes, and I came to the statute for the Levites: "But the Levites are to pitch their tents around the tabernacle of the Testimony. In this way the wrath will be kept from falling on the whole community of the sons of Israel. The Levites are to be in charge of the tabernacle of the Testimony."

A little further down I read, "Yahweh spoke to Moses and said: 'I myself have chosen the Levites from among the sons of Israel, in place of the firstborn, those who open the mother's womb among the sons of Israel; these Levites therefore belong to me.' "

And again I read: "Take the Levites in the place of all the first-born of Israel's sons, and the cattle of the Levites in place of their cattle; the Levites shall be my own, *Yahweh's own.*"

Strangely enough, this made me think of priests. The Levites quite evidently are the "first-born." This statute of theirs simply expresses an ideal, it seems to me, that flowered into the Christian priesthood of today!

Have you meditated on it, my beloved Father? This is a sort of confirmation for one who constantly thinks of the priesthood with so much love and so much tenderness and so much compassion. Obviously, the priest of today must "pitch his tent next to the tabernacle of Testimony." This means, according to my understanding, that he must keep his heart close to the Word of God, to the Gospel of Jesus Christ! The priest of today should remember that Word, for if he doesn't, the wrath of God is going to descend on all the people of God. No priest would wish this to happen.

It tears my soul apart, and I feel swords within me, as I think that more and more priests have left their tents, the sides flapping loudly to a wind that didn't come from heaven! The priests of today, even as the Levites of old, take the place of the first-born, in this case, Jesus Christ! Therefore, I brought with me, wherever I went, the custom of standing up for priests when they enter a room. For, in truth, each one is Jesus Christ. Yahweh said so himself when he spoke of the Levites and their role.

As my meditation continued in this strange Book of Numbers, I realized over again that the Levites (and this means also the modern priesthood) "are his property . . . belong to him."

Somehow, this meditation that took place one night made my prayers for priests more fervent than ever before. I was beseiged with an urgency to implore the Lord to stop the leakage of priests. Everything became so tremendously clear regarding the role of the priests, above all the fact that they were God's special property and hence intensely blessed by him. In his eyes they were his "first-born" and they were to dwell near him in their tents. For what is the altar of Testimony but himself?

As the glories of the priesthood invaded my heart I cried out to the Lord, "Lord, let them see who they are. Don't let them wander away into the dark wind that doesn't come from heaven." But all the time I also knew that God already is trying—sending his grace, his charisms, his love, giving himself to priests everywhere, but that he would never interfere with their free will, the free will he has given all of us. This is fantastic: The All-powerful has put a restriction upon himself and limited his power so that we, the children of man, may truly be free! Incredible, isn't it?

I don't know why I am writing this to you but I think God has chosen you to live close, very close, to the altar of Testimony, to understand better than others that you belong to God, that you are his property, and to know daily in a great depth as time goes by, that you are his first-born. This is given to you so that you might preach it, give it, offer it, in the chalice of the tenderness of your love and compassion to other priests.

Yes, dear Father, this is a very botched-up first chapter of a book. But then, every word was torn out of my heart while I prayed one night for all the priests of the world. No one writes too well with pieces of her heart.

CHAPTER TWO

SHARING CHRIST'S LONELINESS

I want to tell you now of the terrible tragedy that priests leave behind when they become laicized. Oh, I would not dare to interfere with anyone of you should I have the occasion to do so, for each one is making his own decision, I am sure, before the Blessed Sacrament and in the light of the Holy Spirit. But you see, dearly beloved Fathers, I am a little person and I live and work amongst the laity. I wish I could tell you of the tears the laity shed when, as they say, "he went away," of the prayers that they lift to God, and of the terrible loneliness that suddenly descends on parishes when the priest leaves.

I remember the day when there were no priests in Petrograd. In the early days of the Revolution, when things were so unsettled, priests were shot on sight, and so were many other people. The Jewish Rabbis, the Protestant Ministers, the Orthodox Priests, all were shot or "disposed of" in some way.

Alone, a little Catholic parish was still surviving, and those of us who knew about it participated in the middle of the night in the Mass, a very short Mass but still a Mass. One day when the priest had just consecrated the Host and brought It down on the altar, the door opened, a rifle was thrust through, a shot was fired, and the priest fell dead. The consecrated Host rolled off the altar onto the floor. Two soldiers came up then, ground the Host under their heels, and turning to us said, "Where is your God? Under our heel!"

An old man answered, "*Lord, forgive them, even if they know what they do.*" Shamed or embarrassed, the two soldiers left the church. The old man gave us Communion with the remnants of the Host. He washed the desecrated floor with holy water, and we buried the priest.

And then there were none! No one to hear one's confession. No one to give us Viaticum and the last rites (as they were called then.) No one to offer Mass. Anyone who has gone through this tragedy knows what it means to be without a priest. I never thought I would live to see the day when parishes would be closed, monasteries be sold for lack of vocations and departures.

Oh dearly beloved Fathers, there isn't an ounce of criticism in me or of accusation. No, nothing of the kind. All I can do is pray and weep. Russians believe in the gift of tears more than in the gift of tongues, (though they accept the tongues too), for we say that tears wash away so many things in ourselves, in others, and in the world. My prayer is constant, unfailing. I am not afraid to say publicly that it is a prayer of faith. I pray that God quickly send replacements for those who left. And I pray that those who left may find the peace that they sought, or come back if possible.

Yes, I ceaselessly and constantly pray to God to quickly send replacements for the priests who have left.

But there is more that I want to say to you, Father. I want to share with you your loneliness, because it is one of the reasons why you feel so unsure about things, especially as your years in the priesthood progress. I once wrote a poem about loneliness, because I am lonely too. And though, of course, I do not share your presbyteries or other places where you live, I can sense your loneliness.

I will give you the poem, the whole poem. Maybe it will console you a little. Maybe not. But anyhow it will tell you that I share your loneliness.

> Dark as the night
> Is the pain of Christ.
> Dark as the night
> And as lonely.
> Strange as the night

Is the silence of Christ,
And as deep.
Long as the night
Is the suffering of Christ.
Long as the night,
And as endless!

Day stands outside of it,
Crouching and fearful.
For once, it seems
It cannot conquer the night!
For the night holds
The pain of Christ.
Holds his pains and his tears,
Holds his joy,
And will not let go.

Chalice of night,
Will you reveal
To a loving heart
The sight of one tear,
The echo of one sigh,
The one cry of pain,
So that it might
Wipe the tears,
Share the pain,
And gather the sighs
Like an endless refrain.

But the night stands still,
Recollected,
Holding all of it
Unto herself.
For even she will not
Give away
The secret of the
King of Kings.

There is but one way
For a loving heart.
It must enter the night
And weep where he wept,
And sigh where he sighed,
And suffer his pain.

Will you open
The door of your heart,
Dark night,
For a loving heart?
The door is unlocked,
And the loving heart
Now abides
In the heart of the night
That holds it tight
But allows it to move
In the breadth and the width
Of this endless night
That held his torment.

It takes in
All the nights of time
That waited
For this night of nights,
This night
That held
Gethsemani.

Will you lift her up,
Dark night, the loving heart,
And let her in.
Lift her up
And let her cover him
From the sight of men?
It cannot be done.
He has to hang

Naked and alone
On the tree of death,
Like a king on a throne,
With naight but the night at noon
To cover his shame.

The loving heart stands
At the foot of the cross,
Shrouded in the warm noon-night.
She cannot see a thing.
But the warmth of his blood,
She feels,
Falling on the earth.
And some of it brushes her
As it falls
And she knows ecstasy.
And so does the night.

Strong as the night
Is the pain of Christ,
And as deep.
And why shouldn't it be?
For the night gathered up the pain
And kept it in the chalice
Of the dark.
And all who seek him
Must walk to his light
Through the dark of the night.

Well, it is the same with you, dear Fathers. Sometimes in the night in which you walk—for you walk always in the night as well as in the day, in pain and in joy—the same can apply to you.

"Dark as the night is the pain of Christ." So is yours. "Dark as the night and as lonely." So is yours. "Strange as the night is the silence of Christ and as deep." And especially you must feel this strange silence of Christ because just at the moment when you think you need him most, he seems to be absent.

"Long as the night is the suffering of Christ—Long as the night—and as endless!" The same applies to you. Across the ages over and over again, generations of priests have felt that same way: lonely!

I once dreamt that I was brought to a Trappist monastery in the dead of the night, and I passed by the sleeping Trappists. They did not know I was there, such was the dream. But I knew each time I passed by a cell, what was going on: this and that one had cried in the night. His tears were still wet on his face. Another one was in the throws of a nightmare—fighting two thousand temptations that Satan presented. On and on I went, from cell to cell, without entering any, and from each came a whiff of that loneliness I am talking about. From that day on I have always prayed for Trappists as well as for many other Orders.

It was a strange dream, for very soon after that the Trappists of the world began to give up silence, began eating meat, and I imagine then that their loneliness was even more acute, for they were leaving La Trappe, beaten to the ground by that loneliness.

But it doesn't only apply to La Trappe. It applies to all monasteries and all secular priests and everyone else. No wonder you talk so much about celibacy, about joining a community, about some way or other of getting rid of loneliness, the loneliness of Christ.

"Long as the night is the suffering of Christ—long as the night and as endless!" Who wants to enter into the dark night of Christ? Who wants to open his heart to this endlessness, this strange request that God makes of us, and of you especially.

Christ loves his priests. It is incomprehensible to us how much he loves his priests. He loves them like brothers. But what is more, he loves them as himself. Because, you see, a priest is Christ, and the Father loves them because he loves the Son, and the Icon of the Son is in the heart of every priest. And so the Father bends over each heart with a love that surpasses all understanding, and the Holy Spirit sends his fire and flame constantly upon you. You have a Pentecost every day.

It is hard for you to realize this because you usually look upon yourself only as a man. If only you could see yourself as the Father sees you, as the Son sees you, as the Holy Spirit sees you. Yes, loneliness is yours, but don't you understand, dearly beloved Father, that your loneliness is shared with Jesus Christ—with the Trinity. The Apostles were asleep in Gethsemani. But Christ never sleeps. He is always at your side and he shares your loneliness.

Does it ever occur to you, dearly beloved Father, that he also shares with you his joy, providing you look for it? Sometimes we try to grasp the joys of others as a child grasps a red ball that belongs to some other child. This won't work. It won't work because your hands were not made to grasp anything. Your hands were made to bless, to console, to give, to hold the hands of the sick so that they might get well. Your hands are filled with holy oils. It doesn't matter that you wash them everyday or several times a day. Holy oils are impervious to that type of washing. Don't look at the red ball. Don't! Look at Christ—Christ the Child—Christ the Youth—Christ the Adult—Christ our God—Christ who is in you!

It's a stupendous thing, dear Father. I am just an ordinary lay person, but when you come into our house or I go into yours, I feel a sort of complete joy. It's as close as I come to the living Christ. You think I exaggerate? Oh no, not at all. You are the living Christ, in a manner of speaking. He ascended, but he loved us so much—us, his Mystical Body of which he is the head, us, his people of God—that he couldn't possibly leave us. So he left himself *in you*. Do you understand that, Father? Do you?

Yes, he left himself in you, in the Bread and Wine, in the Eucharist. He left himself in Icons and in the Saints and in a lot of ways, but above all, in the Eucharist and you. Only *you* can offer the Eucharist. Remember that. Without you there is no Eucharist.

Men lived without the Eucharist in many places of the world at many times. But those who were Christians always hungered for it. At one time a pastor of a rural church was unable to attend Mass on Sunday. He was sick and he seldom got a replacement. You could feel the sadness and the prayers of the parish for him, asking God to send a replacement.

Do you understand, dear Father, what it means to be without the Bread and Wine for a long time? It means walking through an arid desert with the sun beating on your head day and night. Yes, that is what it means, and much more.

Don't look toward the red ball that belongs to somebody else. Look to the heart of Christ that is yours for the asking—yours for the praying—yours for the dancing! Christ danced. He was a Jew. The Jews always danced ritual or holy dances. (When I was in the Holy Land recently I heard men dancing near the church.) Join in the dance of Christ! Enter his joy. He will be so happy to have you!

True, the loneliness will be with you, perhaps always, but the song of the Trinity will reverberate in your heart and you will be able to dance to its tune. Joy inexpressible will overcome the loneliness.

Loneliness shared with Christ, with a deep understanding as to why you are sharing it, turns to joy. But this is a kind of joy that stays deep within the priestly heart. It remains there. It is like a little brook watering the deserts that are so often in men's hearts, especially priestly hearts.

CHAPTER THREE

CHRIST RE-CRUCIFIED

There seems to be two trends in your life, dear Father. Th
old trend I remember well: There was some inability t
communicate with your bishop or Ordinary. It seems as if you
just couldn't—to use a slang expression—"spill the beans" to
him. But the bishop was and is the Father of your soul. Hi:
attitude might be completely wrong or completely right, eithe
way. But in many cases something stops so many of you from
going and talking to the bishop with an open heart. Yet, I have
found bishops very easy to talk to.

I'll tell you a story of what happened to a priest, long
before Vatican II. He wanted to get laicized. He came to
Friendship House on his free days to teach catechism or to
wash windows or to do whatever was necessary at the time. His
problem was very simple, and he stated it to me often.

He belonged to a parish where the Pastor was interested
mostly in "decorating the parish," if you want to put it that
way—making the church sort of a sightseeing attraction. He
used carrara marble to make an altar. (As you know, carrara
marble is one of the most expensive marbles.) He used a
cheaper marble to decorate the sanctuary. He bought all kinds
of beautiful things. Every week my young priest would sit with
me over a cup of coffee and say, "I can't stand it. I really can't
stand this aggrandizement of the sacristy and everything else,
when in a corner of our parish, although it is a wealthy parish,
there is poverty untouched. Nobody pays any attention to it.
And all these poor people are Catholics." I have forgotten

whether they were Portuguese or Puerto Ricans, but they were Catholics. He said, "When I minister to them, the Pastor resents it. He wants me to pay attention to the Altar Society. They don't need my ministrations at all, the more so that he has a very good priest, another assistant, who likes all the aggrandizement. He seems to take everything beautifully and manages somehow to instill the Gospel in those people. I don't know how they take it, but I shouldn't judge. But the point is I want to be laicized."

I said, "Look, Father, why don't you go to the Cardinal (this was happening in New York) and really lay your soul open to the man. He is a good man. But it doesn't matter if he is good, bad or indifferent in the natural order, he is the Father of your soul, and there's no getting away from that. On top of all that, he ordained you. That's where you should go!

"Oh," said he, "the Cardinal!" And the matter was dismissed by one of those strange "ohs" that trail off with a long ending. So I decided to take the matter in my own hands, which I usually do! I made an appointment with the Cardinal and I said to him, "Your Eminence, you are going to lose a priest because he cannot stand his Pastor's continual decoration of the sanctuary, the church and the rectory to the neglect of the poor. He wants to be laicized, this good, holy priest, and he is a real man. He spends his time with the poor in the parish whom nobody cares about."

So of course, I gave him the name of the parish, the Pastor and the priest. I said, "It's up to you to get the thing straightened out because you are the Father of his soul."

The Cardinal looked at me through half-closed eyes and said, "Katie, one of these days you and I are going to run this diocese." I said, "Oh no, Your Eminence, I can never trespass on those affairs. I can only follow in your footsteps." But you know, I was young and silly, so he laughed and said, "Alright, alright, alright!"

About two weeks passed, and the priest who washed windows and catechized the little Negroes on his free time came and he said, "Catherine! A miracle has happened! A miracle! Literally a miracle! Don't think it's not a miracle. In New York it is a miracle!" I said, "Well alright, Father, tell me. I like miracles." "I have been transferred," he said, "just like that! To the poorest parish. Can you imagine that? Can you imagine that? So, demure like a woman should be, I shook my head and I said, "Yes, Father. The age of miracles is not past, but you should have gone yourself and talked. Somebody must have talked for you." "Oh," he said, "nobody has talked for me. It's a miracle! He was inspired!" I said, "Yes, I think he was inspired," and the conversation ended.

Father, in pre-Vatican II times the priests did not go to their Ordinary because of fear, shyness, or some other reason. But don't blame the Ordinary always. You can always say the Ordinary was busy, or that he didn't call you or something, but you are not going to tell me that you could not knock at the door of your Father and get in.

Suppose that you were in a real big mess in the old days. Well, you could have picked up the telephone, even if it was twelve o'clock midnight, waken the Bishop up, and told him that it was urgent. But of course you never did, or very seldom. So time went on, and the next thing that happened was the post-Vatican II age. Now you don't want to go to the Bishops at all, who are often ridiculed or ignored.

Perhaps, you don't go to bishops because you think you can do without a bishop. But Father, I implore you, I really do: I beg you to understand. Don't forget that Christ gave the fullness of his Spirit to the bishop. You derive your priesthood from the bishop. The very fact that you are a priest means that you are joined to the bishop. True, if you are a priest belonging to an Order you have a Superior who takes the place of the bishop. But you cannot be ordained without a bishop and you owe a special allegiance to the bishop of Rome.

You may not like to have contact with the heirarchy. Yet, in fact, the bishop is the only one who can really tell you the will of God. Oh, most assuredly, your conscience tells you a lot, and your Superiors, but when it comes down to rock-bottom, it's the bishop who tells you the will of God and that is not always an easy thing to hear.

During the reign of Pope Paul VI many wonderful things

were accomplished in the Church. Nevertheless, that heroic man had to suffer many personal wounds and bruises during his service to God's people. Yet, at times, he was highly criticized by the men he loved the most, you his priests. I understand that you are human, you too are men of clay and can commit all kinds of sins just as we lay people can. However, the criticisms leveled at that poor frail man of God by so many of you my beloved priests is difficult for me to understand. So many stones were hurled at him from the left and the right that it is amazing that he was able to serve God's people as long and as well as he did.

Sometimes in the night I feel as if something tragic is happening. I can almost hear the devil laugh. Once a woman was caught in adultery. She was brought to Jesus and was about to be stoned. Jesus turned to her accusers and challenged them with the words, "If one of you is without sin, go ahead and stone her." Her accusers had enough self understanding, self knowledge to walk away. They were aware of their own sinfulness and imperfection. Now, it is not surprising that the Church which is made up of human beings is imperfect in many ways. However, the Church is faithful in her teaching and doctrine and as the bride of Christ remains a spotless virgin. Objectively, the woman caught in adultery was spared by her sinful accusers and pardoned by the sinless Christ. In her spotless heart of doctrine and faith the Church of Christ has throughout the centuries remained innocent. We, who are far from innocent as individuals, should therefore be careful not to stone the Church which gives us life.

The pope cherishes the Church as a whole and each of us as individuals. At night he prays for discernment and during the day for wisdom. Dear fathers, if you truly love the Church, as I know you do, you will unite your prayers with his and neither you nor he will ever be alone in your ministering to God's people. Love is spiritual. It is not thwarted by distances. Being united in spirit with the shepherd of Rome you yourselves will become better shepherds.

Thank God, that lately it has been a little quiet. Perhaps the Church is gathering her rags and sewing them up, because we have torn them and left the rags all over the place. She might be sewing the rags together. Well, it's good to belong to a ragged Church, but it's not good to make the Church ragged as some theologians do!

Enter into this sentence, my dearly beloved Father. Do! Here is the door. Here is the handle, beautifully wrought. Open it...open it. You have spent many years studying all that there is to be studied about God. But do you know the God who is beyond all study, beyond all approaches of the human mind? Have you opened that door? Have you come through it? Once you have, your words, your deeds and your writing mellow and mature.

I beg you, you who have opened the door and entered into the Holy of Holies, be reverent. Theology used to be the mistress of all sciences, and still is to those who understand. But what has happened? What had happened to this pure fountain given by God to man? I'll tell you what happened. Throughout history and in our own time as well, man has put his peanut brain into that pure fountain and polluted it! We are hungry for God as few have been hungry over the centuries. Dear Fathers, give us the truth. Don't give us theology seasoned with *your* salt. It has no flavor. Give us God's theology. Since theology is the study about God then for God's sake pray that God gives you himself, and then you can give him to us.

I told you that many priests don't want to go to the bishops. Some of them don't go because the bishop may tell them they can't do what they want, and some priests, like the hippies, are on a merry-go-round. It goes around and around: "I want to do what I want to do when I want to do as I want to do it."

Well, good and reverend and beloved Father, people who are on a merry-go-round of their own will usually die of hunger and thirst for him who alone can nourish them.

One November night, it doesn't matter in what year, I spent many sleepless hours. I was taken up with a deep inner vision that gripped me without ceasing during that time. There is no use beating around the bush! I was in the throes of a sadness beyond description, a fear beyond the telling of it, a numbness, and yet a clarity of mind that strangely blended together.

It came to me that the Catholic Church was in grave danger. We, the people of God, were a sort of snowball rolling down an immense mountain and in the process became itself immense, and that all this immense mountain of people fell on the Church and crushed it. It laid in ruins underneath the cold snow which seemed to symbolize the cold hearts of so-called Christians.

The conviction grew upon me as the night grew, that the Church is at the crossroads, and that the Church, who is of course us—bishops, priests and lay people—is also the Bride of Christ, the Mystical Body of which he is the head. Yes, the Church is so much more than the people of God.

It seemed to me that this Mystical Body, this people of God, had forgotten, set aside, not taken into consideration the *mysterium* (mystery) of Christ's Headship, and the fact that she is also his Bride.

It seemed to me that we were beginning to treat the Church as if it were only human. We are throwing the Church back and forth as if it were a basketball. At the same time, it seemed to me, in the dark of that night, that so many of us were tearing the humanness of the people of God apart. The conversations were constantly about the errors of the Pope, the priests, the bishops, the nuns, etc., and ourselves too, and our eyes were constantly roaming to find a substitute for what we had deserted.

I realized in that strange night of mine that in some sort of inexplicable way, if we tear that Body, the Head will die. It came to me that the Head will die again, and that we will re-crucify Christ again in ourselves. The word *re-crucify* hit me so hard that I seemed to lose all senses, but they returned, except that with them fear—fear for us who were treating the Church, his Spouse, in such a strange manner. Fear shook me like a fever, for I suddenly understood, heard, the *anger* of the Father at the re-crucifixion of his Son, at this total forgetfulness of

Catholics of the awesome mystery of the Church which is his Son who is at once the Head and Bridegroom.

Our faith teaches us that our God is also a "jealous God." He is concerned, loving of our ultimate as well as our present happiness, tranquility and peace, for God loves man simply because God is God.

It came to me, therefore, that God's anger was just, because we were tearing ourselves apart, destroying our peace. God was angry about our blind, absurd, willful, evil ways of treating the immense graces that he sent through the Holy Spirit. God's anger is always his mercy!

It came to me that God was giving us signs. He was writing some mysterious words on the wall as he did once upon a time in the Old Testament. They were awesome words of warning, of calamity besetting the world, like floods. But more than scientifically explainable words, he was writing on those walls about the terrible, unholy wars that rage, one against the other, in men's souls. For it is in the souls of men that wars begin.

The fragmentation, the division of the people of God, their hostility toward one another, their rejection of the Gospel—these were before me in stark and fearsome clarity during the night.

Of course, I fully understood that the Church will continue to exist and all hell would not prevail against it. Nevertheless, I shuddered and almost wept at the responsibility of my brothers and sisters in Christ, mine and everyone else's. For the ones that tear the Church apart are our elite, people endowed by God with many graces and talents beyond the average. I trembled, I repeat, at their misuse of those talents and their shirking of true responsibility, especially priests. These words came to me in this horrible night of mine: "Woe to them who scandalize the little ones of Christ." The priests, instead of leading the little ones to God, instead of making the way easy for them to find him, were leading them either away from him or confusing them by leading them to themselves.

Yes, there was a Goliath to be killed, but it could only be killed by another David, a simple shepherd boy with a sling-shot of love and the little stones of simplicity, humility and childlikeness as weapons. I saw the priests clad in the garments of service which are the priestly robes of Christ. Next to their sling-shot of love, and the stones of humility and simplicity, they all had a towel and a pitcher of water and a basin to wash the feet of all men who came to them. Those who went down from the mountain of the Lord to the valleys of the world carried nothing with them except the sling-shot of charity, and the pebbles of childlikeness and humility. They were girded with a towel, knowing that they would find a pitcher and a basin and the clear waters of love flowing from their heart wherever they went to witness to Christ.

Yes, such was the strange November night I spent in some unknown year, half-awake, half-asleep.

CHAPTER FOUR

A JOY TO THE WORLD

Dear Father: We have discussed several themes of your priestly life. But there is one that I would like to bring up right now and that is joy.

Do you realize that you are a "joy to the world"? When we sing at Christmas "Joy to the World" and other songs and carols expressing the gladness of the coming of Christ—and then the absolute burst of joy when he comes—did it ever occur to you that the same sentiments, the same feelings, come to our hearts when *you* visit our homes?

In the old days, of course, people prepared for your coming by polishing and cleaning everything. That may have lessened a bit, but today, like yesterday, the *joy* is still there. To have a priest come and visit us—well that's quite something! For those of us who have faith, for those of us who understand a little, it is the coming of Christ. We hear the knock, or maybe it's a bell, and everybody says, "Father is coming," and we rush to the door. This may seem a little old-fashioned to you maybe, especially to the young priests. Even if you don't see these things happening to you, don't kid yourself. They happen in the hearts of the young and the old.

You are a bringer of joy. Even when you come to visit the sick there is some kind of an uplift—some kind of a hope that springs forth. Not necessarily that the sick will not die. No! But some strange, unaccountable joy takes hold of people. Over and over again I have seen it. Working in a hospital, I have seen the faces of patients light up. There was in their eyes an expectancy that you never saw in them before, not even when their husbands or wives, fathers, mothers, brothers or sisters came. It was an expectancy that almost shouted, "Oh, here is Father. I can put my soul into his hands and I can lay my head (figuratively speaking) on his shoulder."

You see, the joy that you bring is manifold, and if you only had time to spend with us you would realize how beautiful it is. If you only had time to look at the faces that your coming creates, you would find yourself praising the Lord with all your soul.

Yes, you are a bringer of joy. Even when you might not bring good news—natural good news—it doesn't seem to matter. You bring supernatural joys.

Suppose, (and I have seen it happen) a priest comes to tell a wife, a mother, a daughter, that her mother has died, that her husband has died, that an accident has happened and the children were killed. How strange this might seem to you because you do not see yourself. How strange that if *you* are the person that brings the bad news of the world, somewhere deep in that broken heart arises the Good News of Christ. Did you ever think about that?

I had a patient who was sick. She was very sick. She always was glad when you came for a few minutes to say hello to her, to hold her hand, to cheer her up. But one day you met me at the door of the ward and you said to me, "I am afraid to walk up to the door of Mrs. So-and-so because I have to give her the news that her husband died. He fell from the fifteenth floor." He was a mason or something. I said, "Father, you must not be afraid because you bring to her the will of God and it will be her sanctification and yours." You looked at me a little strangely, but you went, and you told her, and I was nearby. She screamed. She fainted. We revived her. And she cried. At the end she said, "Well, perhaps Peter is better off, for he is now with God. The Lord said so. He had a good life, Peter. He loved the Lord so he is alright now. It is myself that I should weep for, not him." And there you were, the bearer of natural bad news and supernatural Good News. That is one of your joys, or should be.

But you have so many joys, Father. Do you know their faces? Of course you do, because you have looked into the eyes of the children to whom you teach catechism. Isn't it beautiful to look at the limpid eyes of very young children who have not been touched by the evil of man yet? You must have a voice singing inside of you when you have looked at those children or while you are looking at them, for reflected in the black eyes, the blue eyes, the gray eyes, the green eyes, looking at you is Jesus Christ. What immense joy is yours! And what joy you give to them! Did you ever notice, (unless the Sister is present or some adult who is on the strict side) how they will run up to you and say, "Father! Father! Father!" Just those voices, and the name they call you, must lift your soul up high and allow it to sing as David sang before the altar.

At times, you probably momentarily envy the people whose marriages you witness. The thought of the natural bliss which they share and you have foregone can be painful. Yet, could it possibly be that a strange, quiet and holy joy enters your heart as you bless the wedded pair? Suddenly you realize the very essence of celibacy. Suddenly, as if God opened some kind of door in his own heart, you understand why you are a celibate: because it will light a candle before God on his altar, it will light a candle before his sanctuary.

For a strange moment you see yourself—a candle lit by God. Yes, God has sent the fire, and why did he send the fire but that it should embrace the whole earth. You are the beginning of that fire. A tiny, little light on a candle. You can look at yourself when the bridal couple has departed. You are a celibate. You are virginal. Even if you are a widower, you are virginal at this moment. You are like the virginal wax of the bees, burning yourself up for Christ's sake. Because you are who you are, our heads bow. This kind of chastity for the sake of Christ is holy.

You are the candle of atonement. You are the fire that Christ uses to light in a young soul the heroism which cries, "Lord, I have thrown my life at Thy feet and sing and sing that I bring Thee such a small thing!" This chastity of yours is a fantastic help for the rest of us.

Did you ever realize how the joy of your presence—the joy of being around you—has strangely diminished lately? Some of you have embraced the married state and you have left the altar. I wonder if the memory of what you were has not lain heavily on you.

Something really struck me several years ago. I read a Russian paper in which the priests to be ordained petitioned the Patriarch for celibacy. But the Patriarch refused them because their parishioners would not understand unmarried priests. There were some four hundred of them, so it said in the paper. At the same time I read that many hundreds of priests petitioned the Pope to give them the right to marry!

There is nothing wrong about being married, providing you go through the proper channels. But do you know something, dear Fathers?—the joy that you have now will be different if and when you are allowed to be married. I cannot quite explain this.

Even today somehow, there is an abundant joy—a singing joy—a dancing joy—in the hearts of your people when they know that you have kept the vow of celibacy, come hell or high water. Because they know it is *for them* that you have kept it, and the joy spreads amongst your people because it comes from you.

We need that joy. In the darkness of our age, in the jungle in which we live, we need the candle of your joy, the candle that stands in the candlesticks of faith, love, poverty, chastity and all the things that a priest is or should be.

Yes, Father, you do not realize how much joy your very presence brings. But I wonder if you realize how much *hope* it brings too. As usual, after my many years of contacts with people, I have another story to tell!

I had a spiritual director, Father Keating, a Jesuit. He was then Provincial of the Jesuits in Toronto and lived not far from us on Portland Street, where we had our Friendship House— maybe four or five blocks away—right by the railroad yards. The Jesuits bought the place from the Loretto Sisters who moved uptown. So I went to the place quite often, both for spiritual direction and just to chat a little.

I heard one day that Father was kind of run down and that the doctor ordered him to take a walk everyday, at least for an hour or possibly more. The doctor was rather adamant that it should be done in all kinds of weather except in downpours or blizzards. Outside of that, he was supposed to walk, and the doctor told him how long his walks should be.

Well, I went to commiserate with Father and to cheer him up a little, so I thought; but of course I had another idea. (I always have.) So I said to him, "Father Keating, since you have to walk three miles a day, why not walk in the slums—right where you are." In those days the place was not so polluted. The Toronto air was fresh. And where could he go? Only on the Toronto streets. So he might as well walk where he lived.

He said, "What do you mean that I should walk around this place? I should go out to the park or some place away from here." I said, "Yes and no. There is Cameron Street and you know, because I told you many times, both in confession and out, how I worried about Cameron Street. It is filled with Communists."

Father Keating looked at me and said, "So what do you want me to do?" "Oh," I said nonchalantly (I was kind of afraid, but you've got to look unafraid at all times. It's the best policy.), "it's absolutely indifferent where you walk, so why not walk on Cameron Street? Maybe they will throw stones at you but I am sure they would be very little stones. They won't harm you. And you will bring hope to them, because a priest brings hope. Just your walking down these streets, especially Cameron Street and others where ninety-four percent belong to the Communist party, somehow or other you will bring hope."

He looked at me. Being my spiritual director, he knew me very well. He said, "Catherine, you certainly have this Russian ability of building castles in Spain." "Oh," said I, "I have more! I don't build castles in Spain. I am already making like we are in the parousia. Why not dream about what is inevitably going to happen?" So Father asked me if I was absolutely sure that I would enter the parousia, that is to say, paradise. Perhaps I may enter some other place! I said, "Now, now, now, Father.

You are my spiritual director. Would you consign me to hell?" I said, "Would you consign me to purgatory?" "Well," he said, "a spiritual director never discusses such things with a spiritual directee. So what is it that you want me to do?" Thus we sidetracked the purgatory business neatly as only Jesuits can!

Anyhow, he said, "Okay, I'll walk, but I don't quite believe that I am a sign of hope." I said, "The Lord will show you. You forget who you are. Jesuits, Franciscans, secular priests or Carmelites, you forget who you are or perhaps you don't even realize who you are. I don't know, but this is going to show you that you are a sign of hope." So I knelt for his blessing and disappeared. Thereafter, everyday between four and six, I saw Father walking the slummy streets, but especially Cameron Street, and, as I predicted, little stones, not big ones, hit his coat but never his face or anything like that. A few words about hypocrites and that sort of stuff were thrown out of the windows, but he was six-foot-one, very good looking, and very strong looking. He was about fifty or more. He had presence.

Anyhow, the season went on. Fall came and Fall went. The snowflakes came. One day a woman ran out from a house—little houses they were. She looked around to see if anybody was watching. Then she whispered to Father, "Pray for my son. He is very sick." And she scuttled back again.

Father dropped in at Friendship House and he said, "Maybe you are right. Maybe I am a sign of hope," and he walked out. Well, thereafter the woman came again and again. One day, very quietly, he put a blessed medal in her hand—a medal of Our Lady of La Salette. Then she ran away again.

About a week later she came again, standing straight and not running, not afraid of anybody. She took Father's hand and kissed it according to the beautiful Slavonic custom, and she said "My son is well, thanks to your prayers."

I am almost afraid to say the next sentence, but I have to say it because it's the truth: Do you have that kind of faith? Have you really looked at yourself and understood who you really are? Oh, you might be Tom, Dick or Harry. You might be fat, thin, old or young. You can look in a mirror until the mirror falls down, but you will not see in a mirror who you really are. It's when your eyes are turned to the heart of Christ, which is your real mirror, that you will see that you are another Christ, with all his powers, amongst them the power of giving hope, joy, faith and love.

Yes, believe it or not, when you are around you are a sign of hope. You might not feel that you are. You might not even know that you are, but you are. Be careful! Don't let it slip through your fingers, for the hope of the soul of a human being is a fragile thing, and the laity has been led to so many dead-ends with the slogans, "God is here. God is there. Come here. Go there." All these things have been lies. They will approach you sometimes as if you also were a liar and a hypocrite. Sometimes anger will spill upon you because someone has betrayed the most precious thing: God in a human soul. I am not saying that it happens all the time, but it may happen sometimes.

So remember: you are a sign of hope. You are a sign of joy. You are a person who lives on the street of broken dreams because you lead people to God who alone can repair them. You can do it too. God and you are good repairmen. Perhaps in our century you could call it the "re-cycling of hearts." Be that as it may, you are a sign of hope.

CHAPTER FIVE

HOLOCAUSTS OF LOVE

We have discussed your being a sign of joy, a sign of hope. But we haven't discussed your being a sign of love.

Love is a strange thing. St. Paul has the best definition of love that I have ever encountered. He begins very simply by talking about the order of importance in spiritual gifts. Coming to love he says, "Be ambitious for the higher gifts. And I am going to show you a way that is better than any of them." Now isn't that something, my dearly beloved Father? St. Paul is truly showing us a way that is better than any others. He removes from love all that is not of God, purifies it and makes it holy. He lifts it up. But let's hear what he has to say.

"If I have all the eloquence of men or of angels, but speak without love, I am simply a gong booming or a cymbal clashing." How often has this been true of Christians. How often has it been true of you, dearly beloved Father? Rounded out phrases, beautiful sermons given with eloquence. Why is it that the people did not rush to you, did not thank you, did not surround you as they would have surrounded Christ? They politely passed you by and said, "Charming sermon, Father. Very, very nice," but walked away rather sorrowful. Why?

"If I have the gift of prophecy, understanding all the mysteries there are, and knowing everything, and if I have faith in all its fullness, to move mountains, but without love, then I am nothing at all." Can you imagine that? Can you imagine yourself possessing the gift of healing, the gift of prophecy, the gift of discernment, plus, of course, the seven gifts of the Holy

Spirit? But if you exercised them without love as St. Paul says, "... then I am nothing at all."

Those words are frightening, aren't they, because a lot of us exercise the gifts of the Holy Spirit because they put us in the limelight. They add to our self-glorification. It's the most tragic thing when, given all these gifts to bring others to God, we hug them, in a sense, to ourselves, and take a certain pride in possessing them. Of course St. Paul is right: Then we are nothing.

"If I give away all that I possess, piece by piece, and if I even let them take my body to burn it, but am without love, it will do me no good whatever." Those are very strong words, aren't they, dearly beloved Father?

So love, or "charity" as St. Paul calls it, in all gradations, is the very essence of your being. Because when you possess God, you possess Love. Ordained in his ministry, but even more, ordained in him because he is you and you are him, the one thing you have to give is love. You must give it away abundantly because your hands can plunge, every hour, every minute, every second, into the fathomless, bottomless love of Christ. You must give away the love that God gave us, the love that he exhibited in his Incarnation, passion and crucifixion. It's yours! Yours! To have and to hold for a second! Just for a second, then to give away lavishly because it will come back to you from the very Source from which it came when you were first ordained. So love is what you have to give all the time.

But let's look further. "Love is always patient and kind." I think of the sixties. The gleeful "unkindness" of so many caricatures of the hierarchy, the Pope. Making fun of things that are not funny. The sacred cannot be reduced to the profane. Not at any time.

"Love is always patient and kind." Can I examine my conscience and say that I am patient and kind to authority, to my brethren, to those so-called "beneath me," to the poor, to the humble, to everybody? And yet, my dearly beloved Father, God is patient with you, infinitely patient. You push and you pull and you explain him away in your theologies, and you want to eradicate him in other theologies. Why? Has the source of love dried up? All you have to do is turn your face to God and ask for it, for God is merciful, and no matter how much you hurt him he will immediately restore communication between you and him.

"Love is never rude or selfish; never vulgar." Yet the way we have been treating the whole set-up of the Church, is really tragic, isn't it? And while we did it, guilt came over us. We laughed, didn't we? We thought we were relevant because we joined the group of people who laughed. But did you notice that those groups wept while they laughed? Did you see their tears? They were hidden in their heart, but you, with the gift of discernment, could have given peace to those who laughed at God and at his ministers. God is not mocked, but so many didn't remember that.

"Love does not take offence and is not resentful." It's rather obvious, so why don't those of you who still have a chip on your shoulder against God, why not fall on your knees, put your head in his lap and cry out: "Lord, have mercy on me a sinner!"

"Love takes no pleasure in other people's sins but delights in the truth; it is always ready to excuse, to trust, to hope, and to endure whatever comes." Just read that again. Read it again because it's so important. "Love takes no pleasure in other people's sin." It never points a finger at another, only at oneself. Love naturally delights in the truth because it not only speaks it and thinks it, but knows itself so well and knows that God is always ready to forgive.

You often see the Prodigal Son returning to the Father, and, in confession, you, in Jesus' Name, excuse, annihilate any confessed fault. *Ego te absolvo.* . . . It's not you who is absolving. It's God, but through you his pardon comes again and again. If it comes to your penitents, how about you being a penitent at Christ's feet? I am sure you are because love is like that. It goes there often.

"Love, hopes and trusts and endures whatever comes." Of course it trusts. Above all, it trusts the untrustworthy for the simple reason that you and I are being trusted. We are very untrustworthy, don't you think so, dear Father? With all the blessings, with all the miracles of our being, we are still untrustworthy, aren't we? So if God trusts us we have to trust the other, especially the untrustworthy. Not for us the saying, "Oh, I have just given this chap a dollar and now he is back again with the same excuse." Well, Christ said, "If someone asks you for a coat, give your tunic also." But those who receive it have nobody but you. True, they might go and sell it for a couple of bucks to get a drink, but by now everybody knows that drinking is a disease. You are not going to refuse a sick man a cloak, are you?

St. Paul goes on to tell us that even if I deliver my body, if I have no love, I am like a gong ringing in an emptiness that is not filled with God. Love makes the slightest gesture beautiful and holy. The sharing of a match. The sharing of oneself. The opening of oneself to another. The sharing of a room. The sharing of money with love—all become part of Christ's act. Now you are like Christ, and no one knows what happened to the man to whom you gave that cloak, that dollar or a match. No, nobody knows.

It's rather obvious, isn't it, that the one thing that God asked from us the laity, from the priests, from the Pope, down to the beggar and the prostitute, is to love one another, because through loving one another we love him. That is the quality of love that should above all else interest a priest.

But St. Paul continues: "But if there are gifts of prophecy, the time will come when they must fail; or the gift of languages, it will not continue forever; and knowledge—for this, too, the time will come when it must fail. For our knowledge is imperfect and our prophesying is imperfect; but once perfection comes, all imperfect things will disappear." He continues: "When I was a child, I used to talk like a child, and think like a child, and argue like a child, but now I am a man, all childish ways are put behind me. Now we are seeing a dim reflection in a mirror; but then we shall be seeing face to face. The knowledge that I have now is imperfect; but then I shall know as fully as I am known." All gifts of the Holy Spirit will cease. Love alone will remain. You will appear before God in a cloak of love. I hope so. I hope it will not be a torn rag, but a cloak. It should be smooth and red and beautiful, reflecting the sun.

Your priestly life is a life of love, my dearly beloved Father, and this kind of love that I am talking about now, the one described by St. Paul, deals easily with earthly love. It deals easily with it because you have tasted the love of the Father. You have been immersed in that sea of love that is your ordination. That is the secret of chastity, my friend. The ability to love as Christ loves. That is the secret of chastity.

Remember this when temptations against Love come to you, because that's what they are: temptations against the incredible Love in which you were immersed by the sacrament of your ordination. You can understand the vow of chastity only in that context. Without it there can be no vow of chastity.

But don't you see, dearly beloved Father? Don't you see what happened to you? You are covered with the crimson cloak of God's love. It is crimson because he died for you and me, but you especially, in a manner of speaking. You are clothed with it, for it is like your other skin. You can walk across the road that is laid out for you by God in peace. That strange peace that comes to a priest, I imagine, when he contemplates what the sacrament of the priesthood has given him.

Do you realize what your chastity means to us the laity? I do not want to remind you that the young people in the sixties and even now in the seventies, say, "What is the use of making a commitment when you see Father So-and-So-and Sister-So-and So throwing off the traces?"

Yes, you are a sign of hope wherever you go, but you lift men up to heights unknown when you are chaste. They truly begin to understand what holiness is, and after all, why have we all been baptized in the death and resurrection of Christ? To become holy. We all should be holy, looking at our Head, but especially you, walking in the crimson cloak given to you by Christ at your ordination as a young man. Now we can touch the crimson cloak. Now we too can be chaste according to our state in life. We too can consider chastity which we have thrown away as if it were an old rag.

Your chastity, Father, and others', is the warp and woof of our holiness.

While thinking about chastity and love I suddenly received two other words that seem to supersede chastity and love. The words were *compassion* and *mercy*, and I realized that they, of course, stemmed from love. I began to meditate about these lovely, beautiful virtues.

To me a virtue is an outpouring of a heart. Do you think that is theologically correct, to call a virtue "an outpouring of a heart"?

I must admit that compassion and mercy were very much entwined in my heart. The face of one and the face of the other were like Siamese twins, if you know what I mean. But when I thought of compassion and mercy, I automatically thought of God, because isn't he the All-merciful One, the All-compassionate One!

I discovered something new: I did not know that the human heart can hold a sea of compassion! A brook, a little river maybe. But a sea? No! No, I did not know that the human heart could contain a sea of compassion and of mercy. But I found out quite recently that I can.

One night when I was praying I suddenly saw the wall of my log-cabin vanish (I must have dozed off). Anyhow, it had gone, and my not overly big dwelling was suddenly crowded with priests! Priests filled with doubts. Priests filled with pain—a hidden pain. Priests who were waiting to be laicized. Priests who wanted to marry. Priests who were thinking of divorce. Priests who were staying where they were appointed to stay but looking so very tired. Some of them were positively exhausted!

From my mind and my heart and my soul there suddenly vanished every desire to accuse any of those priests for their lack of faith, weakness, or immaturity. I was suddenly filled with love and compassion. I wanted to take them in my arms as if I were their mother or their older sister. I wanted to console them. I wanted to tell them how much I loved their priesthood which is the one priesthood of Christ. I wanted to tell them how

I and all of us, the laity, needed them. But even our needs disappeared in this love and compassion that engulfed me.

I wish I could speak, write, convey somehow to every priest in the U.S.A. and Canada who is in the throes of doubts, pain, inner battles and weariness, that he is not alone. That in the rural depths of Canada there is one funny woman who loves the priesthood with a love that she cannot understand herself, for it transcends her understanding; but her heart is a sea of love and compassion!

I wish I could sit down and write to every priest in the U.S.A. and Canada that I share his pain, simply share it, whatever pain it might be, because I love their priesthood. They are my brothers and my Fathers and they are so lonely and so lost these days. But I cannot write to every priest in North America. I can simply repeat what I have said before: that the doors of Madonna House are wide open. We have a humble, simple house for priests. We have poustinias, log-cabins where one can be alone with God and rest and can perhaps re-learn how to pray, if this be one of his needs.

Priests are men set apart twice by the Lord. They heard the Lord's voice speak twice, and call them forth, once at Baptism, and then at ordination, to become another Christ. He asked them to arise and go forth into the abysses below, into the man-made hells on earth, and there abide until they are dead, dead to themselves, dead to the flesh, the pomp, all worldly honors, all that men hold dear.

Yes, to arise and go into the abysses of man-made hells where few know his awesome, healing, gentle Name. And there to find Mary who abides in all the hells and haunts of men, because as Mother of God, she also is the mother of men.

Alone she will show them her *house-of-love* where they must dwell. No matter if that "House" is but a hut falling apart, a barge, a house, white, sedate, far from all that the world cherishes. Or, it may be a bamboo hut, a cold igloo, a desert tent. *It still remains her house of love,* and they must dwell there.

These priests will begin their life as holocausts for all the priests who do not share Bethlehem and Nazareth, and would not go to Gethsemani, and the Hill of Skulls. They will be holocausts for those priests who prefer to lead a life of ease with unctuous smiles and holy words spoken with lying lips, who take widows mites to buy TV sets and golf clubs, and who go on luxurious pilgrimages.

They will be holocausts for all the priests who are afraid of men and not of God, for all who revel in pomp and power and are puffed up by it.

They will begin their lives as holocausts. A holocaust is a sacrifice that must be totally consumed, so that not a shred or speck is left. It has become a complete offering totally consumed.

Holocaust and Sacrifice, just like her Son. Passionately, utterly, lovingly, they give themselves as holocausts of *caritas*. For only then will they become men of peace and bring to the man-made hells his peace that no one can or will dare take away from those to whom they give themselves.

But holocaust means death, and die they must. A slow and painful death of crucifixion, just like Christ died for them.

Men set apart by him who is, they shall be known as priests of *love, mercy and compassion*.

CHAPTER SIX

"FATHER, I WANT TO BEGET CHILDREN"

I have spoken of chastity already, but somehow or other the subject won't let me be. I received a letter from a member of a religious order asking me to express my opinion on the subject of "priestly chastity" for the benefit of their seminarians and novices. For women have been asked to express themselves on this rather controversial subject!

So I must admit that when I got that letter I meditated on it. It is the kind of letter that you have to meditate on in order to gather courage, first, and in order to try to answer it somehow or other.

As I thought about it, it became a little clearer why this particular group of priests and some others asked me to write on the subject. Had I not been married twice? Was I not a Russian, very familiar with the whole concept of married priests? For in Russia, Bulgaria and Serbia, all parish priests are married, or they are widowers. True, they get married before they become priests; during their last year in the seminary they are allowed to go and find themselves a wife. Then they get ordained. They can't get married again should the wife die. That's the way it is in the Orthodox Church. I also had an Orthodox mother who could not conceive of a secular priest being "unmarried." She considered that monks alone rated that privilege. So I have been exposed to two points of view.

Then I remembered my case, or perhaps I should say "our case"—mine and that of my late husband, Eddie Doherty. I remember that our case was rather unique in the North American continent, and for all I know, perhaps in the world, for both Eddie and I took a vow of chastity in the fifties, because of the nature of our particular form of Madonna House Apostolate. This demands, by common agreement of its members, a total dedication of one's life to that apostolate through the three promises of chastity, poverty and obedience.

Incidentally, Eddie and I discovered, after years of observing this vow of chastity, that our marital love, the essence of the Sacrament of marriage, had grown to incredible proportions, that our "oneness" with each other had become deep and profound; and that in an incredible way we truly were one in Christ—one in love, in our innermost being. Thus, far from separating us from one another, abstinence of the flesh had brought us closer than either one of us could have imagined!

So I meditated again on the letter of the good priest who evidently had some valid reasons for asking my opinion, for an opinion is all I can give.

I still confess to a certain nervousness, or tension, in tackling this subject. "Chastity," in the mind of the average North American, is frequently associated with sex. But there is so much more to chastity than sex.

Chastity has its birth in the womb of love—*Caritas*. It belongs to the "pure of heart," to those who "shall see God." They shall see God not only in the hereafter but in the here and now.

Chastity is a state of being in which the person abides in the immense tranquility of God's order. Chastity is an identification, a very deep one, with Christ himself. He was "a virgin," which did not stop him from loving men, women, and children with an immense love, or having deep friendships with various men and women, like St. John the Beloved, Mary Magdalene, and others.

We should approach the whole question of chastity in the context of love. I can well imagine, for instance, a group of seminarians, especially on the eve of ordination to the priesthood, either discussing, or simply thinking about marriage.

That is the moment of supreme decision. At this moment, maybe, they almost see the unknown woman who could have been their wife. As the Scriptures might say, they feel in their loins the surge of life, a deeply spiritual surge, that brings before their minds almost palpably the children they might have had: sturdy boys and lovely daughters. Their arms may ache with a desire to hold these children who will never be born of their flesh. Yes, I can easily imagine such thoughts coming to young men on the eve of their Ordination.

But then, if they really face the priesthood in its fullness and its immense grace, they may have other thoughts that will blot out, as it were, the previous ones, normal and natural as these may be. They will remember that "God has a need of men who will help him to seek out and bring to him men who have need of God."

This, truly, is of the essence of the priesthood. For in this tremendous mysterium, young men can behold a miracle of a God who has need of priests, as a paralytic has need of crutches! Incredible simile, yet a true one! The world of souls is, in fact, as hard as stones. The incredible and miraculous situation is this, that a man must give to God his eyes, his hands, his feet, and his works, so that God can, through him, reach other men.

So why speak of sacrifice, of renouncing, of giving up paternity? A true priest is filled with it to overflowing. A poem comes to mind that I read somewhere, written by a priest, which says, "Father, Father, Father, Lord, I want to populate, to beget children for thy kingdom, which begins here on earth and continues in heaven. I want to fill Thy kingdom with the sons of my hands, baptizing, forgiving and giving bread. Thus shall I see Your immense mansions filled with my sons, and the sons of my sons, and the children of the sons of my sons."

This brings me to the current idea that marriage is a short-cut to "personal fulfillment." It may, and it may not be. Moreover, if one seeks marriage in order to *be* fulfilled, or to put it another way, in order to satisfy one's emotional and psychological needs—the clear answer is that it would be a terrible mistake for a woman, a layman, or a priest to marry. Vocations demand maturity, emotional maturity that doesn't seek to "fulfill itself," but seeks to give—"give and fulfill the other." This is the vocation of marriage.

I feel so uneasy when I read the reams of printed words written on the subject of celibacy or chastity, as well as the arguments in favor of married clergy. Do they think that marriage is really the solution to their problems? If so, they know very little about marriage. They should consider the host of problems every married couple has to face.

Russian secular priests were married, and still are married men. So are most priests of the Eastern Rites. Perhaps, it would be interesting to make a sociological survey of all available Eastern Rite priests, and find out how many would like to be celibates. I personally know quite a few.

Closer at hand, and just as interesting, would be a like survey of Anglican priests who are married.

Marriage and celibacy in the Christian Church, especially the Catholic one, is a matter of discipline. Disciplinary measures can always be changed. But these should not be changed in a time of crisis, nor under the impact of emotionalism, destructive criticism, immaturity, or ignorance.

Christ raised chastity and celibacy to great heights. They are deep spiritual signs that our sex-mad world respects, even though it verbally might deny that inner respect.

It is to be noted that while the Catholic clergy is in the throes of a deep malaise and controversy, the pagan countries continue to respect, love, and imitate those who dedicate themselves in total chastity in the thousand Ashrams of India and throughout the Asiatic world.

God, the Lord of history, prepared the way of chastity long before he sent his Son to redeem us. Chastity was well understood before Christ came. The Greeks and the Romans, founders of our western civilization, knew the meaning of chaste virgins dedicated to the temples of their gods.

Chastity is found along that strange journey inward that

man must undertake to meet the Triune God who dwells within him. When that happens, chastity will become the priests' guide and show him all the shortcuts to passionate love of God, and men—a love free and untrammeled of any consideration other than the will of the Beloved.

Then the souls of such men, such priests, will soar to the heights of Love; and they will indeed bring Christ's kingdom to the earth.

There was a young man that sat on the edge of a chair, and tried to tell me stumblingly, and very shyly, that he had finally made up his mind and was going to leave for the seminary in a week or two. Once again my heart stood still, and I felt that strange exultation which always comes to me when I hear told, in halting, shy words, the greatest love story that has come to dwell on earth! The love story of God and man. It happens when the Lord of Hosts bends very low and embraces a heart, and lifts it up high until it reaches the infinite heights of Calvary and the cross, and becomes there—Oh! miracle of miracles— another Christ.

Yes, the young man sat on the edge of the chair and tried to tell me, stumblingly and shyly, that he had finally made up his mind to go to a seminary, and I thought: thirty-one such young men have gone from Friendship House to answer the call of that love, to mount the three short altar steps that change an ordinary youth into a priest of God.

Then again I thought of how many talked to me, without staying very long in Friendship House or Madonna House or any other place. They were just moved to share with me the joy that was in their heart.

Yes, here was another one. No wonder my heart stood still for the space of a second or two. And then gently began to sing an Alleluia, that one-word song which alone seems to be able to express the inexpressible joy of one's heart before God's goodness.

Once again I felt that tremendous surge of love that fills my heart at the thought of the priesthood and priests, for I love it and them with a great, deep, abiding love. My days are filled with prayers for them, or perhaps I should be more specific and say one and the same prayer for them—that on their deathbed, with St. Paul they may truthfully say, "*I live not, Christ liveth in me.*"

As my young man went about his preparations for the seminary I kept thinking of the long, long road he had to travel before that day of days—his Ordination! I thought too of all the temptations, disillusionments, doubts that would follow him into those hallowed walls, and at times even surround him there, and my heart ached for him. For well I knew that the kind of a priest he would be depended so much on the kind of seminarian he would be.

His journey to the summit of love had to begin now, from the first day of his arrival there. For his was a tremendous grace. To be called to the priesthood always is a grace, but at this time of history it is a double grace. For today this vocation includes the possibility of martyrdom, physical pain, unadulterated *martyrdom*. Great love and great spiritual preparation are needed to answer that call, and there is so little time for both. Yes, his journey to the summit of love has to begin now.

Did my young man understand that? Did he realize that Christ was bidding him to go out into the world much like he himself had lived in, or even worse?

My young man would have to deal not only with pagans who were what they were because the glad tidings had not yet been preached to them, but also with pagans who had heard the Word and had rejected it! And what was still worse, they would have to deal with men baptized in the name of the Father, the Son, and the Holy Spirit, who not only denied their allegiance to the Triune God, but who had set out to destroy him in the souls of their fellow men, and who for this purpose had embraced atheistic Communism, or simply atheism, with its credo of irreligion, its apostles and martyrs of hell.

My young man would have to face too the tepidity, indifference, complacency, the secularism and materialism of Catholics already infected with the strange virus surrounding them. All this had to be done against the backdrop of A-Bombs and H-Bombs that foreshadowed complete annihilation.

Indeed, he was being called to the very summit of the holy vocation to the Priesthood, for it was to be lived out in a world poised at the edge of the darkest abyss mankind ever had to face in the long course of its history.

There was only one answer to all this challenge: He had to learn in the seminary not only the ways of being a priest, but the ways of being a saint! Nay, more that that, of being Christ himself!

He had to remember too, that he was being ordained for the people. Without the sheep, there is no need of a shepherd. Thus from his very first day in the seminary, he had to begin dying to self utterly, so as to be ready to give up his time, his health, and his life, for those whom tomorrow he would lead to God.

As I looked on the sorting and the packing my young man was engaged in, I felt like suggesting that he should travel light in order to keep up with the companions of his journey: Poverty, Obedience, Chastity. They demand rigorous training, and a light pack. Theirs are swift and long steps, which exact every ounce of one's energies, none of which can be diverted into other channels.

People today are indeed weary of words. Atheistic communism gains adherents because we Catholics talk too much. We have indeed a lot to say—but we should begin to say it not with words but with deeds. We must preach the Gospel without compromise, and with our bodies as well as with words. If men are to believe in him who sends him, my young man must *show* them the poverty, the obedience, the chastity of Christ, and that means becoming naked out of love for God and neighbor—to follow a naked Christ unto the bitter end. How many suitcases does nakedness need?

As I read his list of various requirements for entrance I felt like writing out another one to hand to him on his first day of arrival, and it would go something like this:

1) Bring out of the seminary with you the knowledge of prayer so that you can teach it to us, your spiritual children to be—the prayer of the Mass, the prayer of meditation, the prayer of contemplation, the prayer of speech, the prayer of

silence, and the Jesus Prayer. We who live in the desert of darkness need to know how to pray more than we need water and food. But we will not accept your booklearning, only your soul-searching. We will learn to pray if you have prayed yourself.

2) Remember too, that we, the laity, each one of us, are a trinity that cannot be rent asunder. For we are composed of body, mind and soul, and you cannot cater to one without taking care of the other two.

Thus when we come to you with our daily problems, as we should, for all of them come under your saintly jurisdiction, (for all have a moral dimension, which is your special field), be ready to receive us graciously, advise us fully and patiently, for who else can?

3) For this, start studying now, diligently, not only the matter specifically related to your future holy state and office, but the whole width and breadth of the social teachings of the Church. Do not presume that these are "not too important" and that you will pick them up some day after your ordination; it would be a fatal mistake, for then you would have forgotten (God help you) that every word Christ uttered, every gesture that he made, *had a social significance so great that it changed the whole world and is still doing so.*

4) Remember too, that the most forlorn, the most degraded among us *have been created in the image and likeness of God,* and that whatsoever you do, or leave undone in relation to us, you do or leave undone in relation to Christ. So don't try in the seminary to find ways or means of "passing the buck of charity." Don't become cynical, and fail us. Please don't!

5) Do not take too literally the saying that you are "set apart." Indeed, so you are, but you have also been ordained to be in the *midst* of us, even though not of us. *Be seen much and often.* The sight of you is a blessing, a shot of new courage to us, a reminder of him who once walked simply and easily amongst the likes of us.

Be approachable, for how will you lead us to Christ if you barricade yourself behind the walls of a rectory and bid us to see you only at certain specific times. We may need you "in between" times. Christ had no office hours. Why should you?

6) *Be heard,* not only from the pulpit, but always. Visit us in the privacy of our homes, on the street, in season and out of season. Tell us about God and the ways of God.

7) Especially be diligent in seeking out the *one lost sheep.* Sinners and the lost ones should be your main concern. Never forget that you *are the shepherd of all the sheep in your parish,* not only the Catholic ones. As Dostoevsky says: "We must love a man even in his sin. For that is the semblance of Divine Love and it is the highest love on earth."

Thus ran my thoughts as I watched the young man packing his grip at Madonna House and making ready for the long journey of ascent that lay before him and of which he as yet knew so little.

Slowly I wended my way to our little white Church by the big river. There I knelt for a long time before Our Lady's altar, imploring her to make him *another Christ,* no matter what the cost, so that beholding him, this hopeless world of ours might once more arise and walk, even as the paralytic, in *faith, hope and charity* toward the wounded Heart of her Son and there be made whole again. *Alleluia!*

CHAPTER SEVEN

GIVE US GOD!

The hunger of men for God is rising like a tide, a tide that nothing can stem; the answers must be forthcoming. Either *we* answer or someone else will. People seek God everywhere. The hippies used to travel across the continents and to India to find him, although now the hippies have disappeared. But the hunger of men has not. Youth still travels across continents to find God.

People travel far and wide to find him, but hunger meets fear. Strangely enough, the fear is in the men who have been touched by God in a very special way, either in the Protestant Ministry or in the tremendous Sacrament of the Priesthood in the Catholic Church. It is to those men that we, the laity, look to, imploring, beseeching, for the answers. We feel we have to have someone "give us God." By this we mean giving us the Word of God.

How does a man, a person, give God to another? Well, for a moment, let us look at the fear of the men of God. They seem to have lost face in their own minds. They are looking for their identity. They are seeking what they call "community." But do they seek the Alpha and Omega? The first Community that we Christians should be one with, but especially the men of God, is the Holy Trinity. The immense and incomprehensible, mysterious, awesome, compassionate Community of the Most Holy Trinity.

Once we enter into the fire and flame of this Community, then, as Christ has said, we shall perform miracles as great as he has done, and greater. One of the great miracles that a human being can perform is to *preach the word of God!!!*

In the east, Christ is Incarnate especially in the Blessed Sacrament, and in the word of God—the Bible. The man who preaches the Word of God is a miracle of God's grace because he doesn't do the preaching, *God* does. And the first step is to be one with God, to be a Sobornost* with God.

What do we hunger for? Long sermons? Explanations of theological or doctrinal matters or the Catechism? NO. We hunger to be taught, to be led, to be healed by the Word of God, by love. Teach us how to love. Teach us true knowledge. Teach us how to pray.

Do not satisfy just our intellects. Teach us not only *about* God but how to *know God himself.*

Teach us how to love, to know *God.* He is not exactly found in books, except one Book.

Help us to know *him.* God reveals himself to those who love him with an open heart, who listen to his words which now come to us like a whisper of a spring breeze, now suddenly in a terrible storm which tears us apart!

Don't be afraid. Don't seek your "identity." You have it! You are a man touched by God, and we, the laity, know it. Do you?

Don't be afraid. We love you, even when we seem to be hostile to you, and when we seem to castigate you. It is simply because some of us think you have let us down, but don't be afraid. You can't be afraid, remember? You have been touched by God, and so it is not you who speaks, but it is he who speaks. Let us hear his voice and we shall know him. We shall not know *about* him as well as you do, intellectually, but we shall know *him* because you gave him to us, and you allowed him to speak through you.

But how is this going to happen if you are looking for your identity all over the place? If you are so busy seeking a community? If you are thinking of "interpersonal relations"?

I cannot understand what "interpersonal relations" are unless I have first a very deep interpersonal relation with the

Most Holy Trinity, with Jesus Christ, my Brother, and with Mary, my Mother.

We speak much of community these days. You are a member of the people of God. You are in a community. The community loves you, and expects from you not eloquence but that "something else" which is more than eloquence, more than the mere polish of words and of sermons prepared three days in advance. No, it is more than that. It is words that come from your heart because you have listened to *his* heart. Then we know that he speaks through you.

I am thinking now of a Man sitting on a green mountain, talking to people who couldn't read or write, mostly cooks and slaves and uneducated people. The educated ones didn't sit on the grass. They may have stood apart but they didn't listen because they didn't have ears to hear. We the laity have a heart that is hungry for God. Give us that knowledge of God which came to you when you were alone with him in his immense silence.

If you ask a Russian what is prayer he will say, "To stand still before God so that you can talk to men." Give us that knowledge. I do not care if you stutter. I couldn't care less if you are afraid a little. Who wouldn't be afraid to stand there in faith, in a darkness that surpasses all understanding, and open his mouth. But he said, "Open your mouth and I will fill it." A little fear is the beginning of wisdom!

Teach us God, because you have met him in prayer and in the study of the Word. The Word is like a tremendous, mysterious teacher. You might be a Scripture Scholar, familiar with every passage, but if you read it on your knees the light of the Holy Spirit will fall on a Word and it will open itself before you like a flower or a nut cracked by an immense nutcracker.

Teach us how to know God, because *you* know him. Teach us how to pray because *you* are men of prayer. We shall know if you are or not, you do not have to tell us, for we are your flock and you are the Shepherds, and we know your voice, and we know *you!*

We know you because he told us that he loves children and

we are children, in a way. Don't pay attention to our present sophistication. The laity today are rambunctious. They go around scratching you here and putting a knife in your back there, or they might seem to. Well, I would like to come with the oils of my love and the wine of my compassion to heal your wounds, for I know some of them are deep. But even then be joyful, because look what the laity of his time, the priests of his time, the whole setup of his time did to Christ!

Maybe your very insecurity is a sign he gives you to turn to him and not to a thousand psychological, psychiatric and other remedies. Nothing wrong with these, but in proper proportion. They will not answer the hunger in your own heart, for your hearts are hungry to give us God just as our hearts are hungry to receive him. You know deep down in your soul that that is why you were touched by God, to give us God!

Don't be afraid. Teach us how to love, and here we come to the sixty-four dollar question: Is love an emotion? Is love a state? Or is it a Person? It is the person of a Carpenter who spent thirty years in a village of no account just making tables and chairs for the villagers. There were three years of preaching, which at the time did not make much impression on the powerful, and not too much impact on the middleclass. He preached. His voice and Word were like a seed in the wind. The megaphone of the centuries carried him into the world, and still does and always will.

What is love?

Some say you have to be married to know how to love. I have been married twice. Do I know love? Well, (I tell you because you are who you are) I know the ecstasy of the flesh, indeed I do, but one Communion, one reception of the Body and Blood of the Lord is ecstasy beyond understanding. The penetration of this tremendous Lover into my soul leaves everything else pale!

Teach us how to love a Person, because love is a Person. Until I, your child, part of your flock, have met him who is love, through you, through the Word that you will preach to me, that you will share with me, I shall not know what love is, celibate or married. It will be something, but it will not be him who is the source of all love.

Reveal the Lord to us from your knowledge of him and your understanding of who you are. Do not be afraid to tell us what is in your heart. Russian spirituality says, "Put your mind in your heart and the world will hear you." I am not theologian enough to tell you, but there is a book that can explain it: *The Art of Prayer*. Eastern Spirituality is very much "in," in case you didn't know it. Basically there is neither Eastern nor Western, but just Christian spirituality. So teach us how to love. Teach us how to pray. Teach us how to understand.

You are so unsure today, insecure somehow, and in a way, so frightened. Yet, "Where two or three are gathered in my name, there I am." He is here and everywhere. "I live not, Christ lives in me." Funny words aren't they, yet that is what we are hungry for. We don't care if you are fat or thin, good looking or not. We don't care anything about that. Teach us about God.

What is there to be afraid of? Tell us stories as he did, the simpler the better! We might be a Ph.D., we might be a lay theologian, but when you tell us parables like he did then we shall know the Truth, and the Truth shall set us free. And you will be free because in telling parables you disappear and he appears.

I have so little to offer you except a tremendous love for the priesthood. You talk about what are called "interpersonal relations." He who loves knows all about "interpersonal relations." He loves everybody because Christ said, "Love ye one another." When you love someone you have an interpersonal relation. You are called to love thousands in your life. With each you are to have the interpersonal relation of a man who leads other men to God. That is interpersonal enough!

Today the Bishops are still our whipping posts—less than before, but still whipping posts. The priests and the laity—everyone—is trying to hit someone else. Why? Even the Pope does not escape this ire. Where is charity? How can you preach

it when there is no charity in all these discussions? I don't care
how violent they get. Please don't be pacifists who go around
trying to stop a war while hitting your own brothers. Let us
begin at the beginning.

How can you preach the Word of God, and how can
anyone listen, if my heart and your heart or anybody's heart is
full of anger against the Bishop, against another priest, or
against another lay person? Before you partake of the Holy
Species, go and make peace with your neighbour; otherwise
you blaspheme the Body and Blood of Christ.

I wish you could hear the laity that loves you and the
Bishops, and the Pope too. Why don't you rest in our love? The
Father, Son and Holy Spirit dwell in our hearts. Preach the
Word of God to us.

I don't know much about Canon Law, theology, and all
those things, but I know something about love. Make it short.
Make it simple. Talk to us about our hunger and your hunger
and tell us that he who speaks through you can heal us and
assuage this hunger. We will respond and come to you because
you are Christ, especially when you preach the Word, his word.
You can heal us and you can assuage our hunger. Eloquence is
not important. Sincerity is, truth is and yourself speaking the
truth.

Foolish of me perhaps, to say that the clergy—Protestant,
Catholic, Rabbis, everyone—needs *prayer* above all. Stand
still before God so you can speak to us. Open your heart to him
and you will be preachers that children will follow on the street.
Give us God and *we* shall go into the ghettoes. We shall clean
them. We shall love. We shall work. We shall pray, because you
have given us the knowledge of how to do it. Yes, you have
shown us because you have seen and felt and touched who you
are and who he is. Because of that we will have touched and
known and fallen in love with him who is love. You will send us
forth like a thousand sparks of fire of the Holy Spirit who
dwells in you.

Remember, you are a priest. Don't try to be someone else
because you think it is easier. There is only one way to come to

us and for us to come to you and that is through his cross which stands forever bathed in a light that is almost blinding.

We are living in the resurrected Christ, not in the dead One. Christ is in our midst now and forever. Give us that light! Give us that joy! Give him to us and your identity crisis will be solved and you will have the Community of the Most Holy Trinity of which you are a part. Your "interpersonal relations" will be a song that we all will hear.

There is a song of silence that man hears coming from the heart of other men. It is all so simple, so simple, my dearly beloved Father, to fall in love with God, to be one with this great Community of the Most Holy Trinity. Stand still before him so that you can speak to men, since God has spoken to you. Then we shall renew together the face of the earth, because love is the only thing that can do it in this time of hate, strife and misery. Love speaks all languages.

It is so simple and humble because the one and only priesthood of Christ is so powerful. I am a member of the people of God, a member of his Mystical Body, one of your flock, and I say to you today, when the Church lies almost prone, her garments seemingly torn, I say to you: Teach us to understand. Teach us how to pray. Teach us how to love. You will know, because *you* love, *you* pray, because *you* are one with him. Speak to us in any way you wish, because he will be speaking in you. Remember: let *him*.

I pray without ceasing for you, for in my poverty I can do nothing else. I beg you, start with him, and all the rest shall be added to you.

---

*Russian word for "unity." Cf. my book *Sobornost*, Ave Maria Press, 1977.

CHAPTER EIGHT

CRY TO THE LORD FOR HIS CHURCH!

For quite a long time now I have been meditating on the role of the laity and the priesthood with regard to the Church. There are two aspects which stand out in this meditation. One is that an institution doesn't need to be bureaucratic. The question is—how are we going to re-Christianize institutions? That is one question that is always on my mind. But deeper, much deeper—before we come to the question of re-Christianizing institutions—comes the question of re-Christianizing the Church!

Now the situation is this. When one says "the Church," one thinks of the hierarchy, the Pope, the bishops, the priests, nuns, etc. But the Church, of course, includes all of us—the people of God.

Now it seems to me that you who are our shepherds and our leaders, will lead us, or should lead us, toward this re-Christianizing of the Church. You probably share my fear that the powers of evil are moving people away from the Church, even though lately the power of prayer has brought many fallen away people back to the Church. Still, there are those who have ceased to believe. Yet, they are members of the people of God. There are millions of them. And what are we all doing about it, especially what are you, priests of God, doing about it?

Now the Christian brings Christ into every aspect of life, into every part of existence. Asleep and awake, he is a Christian: "I sleep and my heart watcheth." What I want to express is not easy. In fact, I find it difficult because all those words are so amorphous and very hard to set out clearly.

Okay, let's begin again. Does God want us to defend the Church as, for instance, in the Crusades? No, I doubt that he wanted the Crusades, but I don't judge past times. We must defend the present Church as it really is, not as men have mangled it, twisted it, and turned it upside down. The Church is a strange, incomprehensible, untouchable, incredible, unassailable mystery that brings men by baptism into the very Body of Christ. Having died with Christ and having risen with him, the Christian becomes one with the Trinity. Who can express *that* mystery? Who can do something about it by himself or by herself? It comes from God. We call it zeal: "Zeal for my Father's house burns in me like a flame."

The Church is the Mystical Body of Christ. Christ is in agony, always, in his Church, and so the Church is a mystery of pain, of agony. The Church is a mystery of joy which believers experienced during the fifty days after Easter in an exultant manner.

The Church is the Bride of Christ—spotless, without wrinkle. The Church is you and I—full of sin and sorrow, evil and good! The Church is human because her Founder became human. Or perhaps you can say it another way: because he became human, the Church, although also human, at the same time was divinized by him.

"By this you shall know that you are my disciples. Love one another as I have loved you." There is some kind of fantastic mystery that is presented to us! To love God as God loves—this is what God is offering us!

But right now there is the human Church—and that human Church is you and the hierarchy. I read some years ago how a woman was stabbed in the streets of Brooklyn. A lot of people were watching from the windows. I am afraid that there is an awful lot of people who are watching the Church and hoping that it will be killed some place, in some corner, somewhere—and perhaps forever—and that no one will go to its rescue, as no one went to that woman who was killed in the sight of so many.

That cannot be! This is the moment in our lives, in our Christian lives, in which we must arise and be inflamed with "the zeal for our Father's house." We have the Advocate in us, the Wind that fans this flame that the Scriptures talk about.

It is time, yes, it is indeed time. I feel like imploring, like weeping, like crying out, like doing a thousand things that men do when they feel close to despair, except that I can't come close to despair because I live in hope.

But I am human, and so I cry out, and I think that lay people cry out with me. Do you hear us? It's not enough to speak softly anymore. We have to cry. So, filled with hope, yet not far away from despair, I howl.

Howl, my soul, howl!
Cry to the Lord, for his Church!

Howl . . . my soul, howl!
For you are plunged in the agony
Of his Bride!

Look! See how she is torn asunder!
How her members mock,
Ridicule her,
Laughing their hellish laughter
As they trample her
Into the mire of their twisted souls!
Howl, my soul, howl
Before the Lord
As tortured men howled on medieval racks!
For those who are thy people
Are trying to make a Harlot
Of thy Bride!

Howl, howl, howl, my soul!
Cry out the agony which is hers
For you are she!

Howl, my soul, howl,
Like men lost in the desert
Howl before dying of thirst!

Howl, howl my soul, howl!

Howl!
The time "for crying out of our depths"
Is past.
The time for HOWLING is NOW!

For men are deaf to all words.
Deaf to the crying and weeping
Of other men!
Yet perhaps the Howling
Of a soul in agony for your Church
Will reach them.
For, as yet, here in this country of the empty rich,
Howling has not been heard yet!

So howl in a whisper
Like a Hindu dying of hunger.
Howl in a whisper
That in its loudness
Enters the mystery of your Passion.
Circling a world which says
You are dead!

Howl, my soul, howl.
Like a woman howls
At the bedside of her lover or child
When she is past speech or tears!

Howl, my soul, howl!
So that the Lord
May hear the song of pain, agony
Beyond human agony
For it is you who will be howling in me.

Howl, my soul, howl!
For the Church is in pain.
Look, she lies in the dust of a thousand roads.

No one stops; the Good Samaritan is not seen
At the bend of those roads yet!

Howl, my soul, howl!
Ask Yahweh
To give you the strength
To lift the Church
Into the arms of his Son.

Howl, Howl my soul, howl!

We are in a diaspora, and yet we don't *have* to be. We are
joined together by the Holy Spirit because we are baptized,
because we have partaken and are constantly partaking of the
Eucharistic Banquet; because the kiss of Christ, in the
Sacrament of Confession, kisses us clean again, and again, and
again, a thousand times over.

So how is it that we are not gathering our forces together
to counteract the strange forces that continue to infiltrate into
the Church, which arise even from within the Church to
manipulate the Church. There is one way in which it can be
done, and only one way: the way of holiness. For this we were
born: to be holy. We are given every advantage by the Church
to follow the path of the Holy One who calls himself "the
Way."

The priest is a shepherd. He has a flock given him by God.
For this he was ordained. God asks from his priests one thing:
that he himself cleanse his soul, that he walk the path of the
Holy One, now falling down, now bruising himself, but since
the path is made by God, God is around and he will help the
priest to stand up and to continue walking.

At the same time the priest must take a broom and sweep a
path for God, so that when we, your flock, listen to you, we
don't have to hear *your* ideas but *God's* ideas. For this you have
been ordained.

It is almost impossible to express the anguish, the agony,
the love that many of us, the laity, feel for the Church. We

know that the Church is us. But we realize (because many of us have been in the business world, have been married, have been in all kinds of positions of authority and subjection) that we need *leaders*. We need you such as you are, as far as your humanity is concerned. I repeat again that it doesn't matter if you are fat or thin. It doesn't matter if you have a beard or not. Nothing matters except that *you know,* and *you show us that you know who you are.*

Nothing matters except that you cease to look for your roles, for your identity. (You are still doing this in the seventies as you did in the sixties.) You *have* an identity; you *have* a role. As long as you are looking for these things we will be left in the desert under the hot sun with no water, and there will be no manna.

True, God will come himself and he will console us, but he will weep over you, because, like St. John the Baptist, you must decrease as human beings; you must increase in him and he must increase in you!

It is time, especially in this culture, that we cease trying to prove something. A priest wants to prove that he is useful. A priest wants to prove, these days, so many things. He wants to be relevant, productive. He has so many words that really don't mean a thing, that pass through one of our lay ears and out another. For a while we listen and say, "Yes," and then, through prayer or even without conscious prayer, people begin to feel that something is wrong. What is it? What is wrong?

There is a pain which almost surpasses all other pain: The pain of watching a priest forget who he is. It is the pain of crying out to him who does not hear: "Look, we don't want you to be a psychiatrist. We don't want you to be a great theologian. Come, help us to protect the Church, which is ourselves and you and the hierarchy. You cannot now teach us the love of God; you cannot teach us the law that Christ brought to us all, because you hate the Bishop and you show it, because you imagine yourself to be a radical in the popular sense, when you should be a radical in God's sense."

God knows I have known radical people; I knew them in their youth. When Dorothy Day and I were in New York—she in the Bowery and I in Harlem—those radicals who even now are attracting some of you came to visit us. There is nothing wrong with their being radical: it is the *way* they do it! True radicalism stems from the word "radix" which means "root." So if your roots are deeply planted in the Church, it is wonderful to be a radical. But if your roots are in the sand of your own ideas or somebody else's ideas, the first wind will blow them off and you will be like grass that flourishes for a moment, then dies the next moment.

I saw an article written recently by a priest that gave me joy, in which he said it would be better if, before priests started throwing stones at the bishops, they looked into their own hearts and questioned themselves. Well, that was a good article!

How can you teach me to "love my enemy" if you publicly attack your Bishop or your Superior whom you consider to be your enemy? No one amongst us wants to enter into any difficulties that you may have, as such, with your superiors, but all of us who love the Church weep when you break the law of Christ. We don't know where to turn any more! The shepherd is not there, and the sheep are kind of huddling together, in the rain, in the snow—and it's cold!

Man's heart hungers for unity, for love, and priests are in demand everywhere. Even young people understand this somehow and are looking for God and for priests.

St. John of the Cross knew what it was to be a spiritual director. A spiritual director is a man who is open—crucified in himself—and who is listening, who has already cleansed the road with his broom for Christ to pass through. He is a man who is listening to the Holy Spirit who tells him, "Listen! Do not preach yourself but give us God. For this you have been ordained." If you understood the depth of the need that we have for you, which is almost impossible to explain, you would begin to understand our cry for understanding. You would understand my poem, "Howl, My Soul, Howl!"

My heart tells me, and it is almost an obsession, that we must get together to protect the Church. There doesn't seem to be many of us, considering the millions that have almost left, but then we must remember that twelve, only twelve, conquered the world. In faith and in hope and in love we must continue to protect the Church, to build it up. But how can we do it? By loving one another, and showing it! By humility, by weakness, by poverty, by the Beatitudes! This is the only way we can protect the Church; there is no other way. In a word, we must live the Gospel without compromise. That is the Church's protection: *for us to really be Christians.*

When I say we must protect the Church I simply mean that we must realize with every sinew of our body the words of Christ: "Without Me you can do nothing."

Night and day, pounding into my heart, are the words, "This is the hour." You see, we have already lost the working man in many places of the world, and we are certainly not welcome in the mission field these days. Right now we don't even know if we can stay in any missions.

But all this is bigger than all the things I am talking about. The Church which Christ founded through his Incarnation, death and resurrection will live forever, there is no question about that. But have *you* the right, as a priest, to send it into the catacombs as so many of you seem to be doing right now?

For me to write these things to you is to show you a love that is beyond any explanation. There are no words in my vocabulary to tell you how much I love you. I cannot explain the unexplainable. I cannot even understand myself, but all the time, beating against my ears like a tom-tom I hear, "This is the time, this is the time. Nothing matters. The fact that you are a woman . . . not the fact that you belong to a little, unimportant apostolate. Nothing matters! Speak out! tell them!"

Tell them what? What can I tell you? Incoherent words, pieces of ideas that come and go in my mind, in my heart and soul. But I must express it because the Church is in danger, grave danger. That is to say, its members are in grave danger of being alienated from God, and that is the greatest sin there is. There is no other. To fall out of love with God is the greatest sin.

Your role is to tell us how to pray, how to love, how to hope. Your role is to show us the tenderness of Christ, his compassion, and his mercy. This is what will protect the Church. This is what will bring about its rebirth. Nothing else will. Not your learning, nor your genius. No. This does not affect it. Only God's truth as it comes through you, as you yourself have agonized over it, prayed over it, gone into the darkness of faith and come out with joy. *That* will teach us, *that* will protect the Church, and *only* that!

That the same can be said to the laity is perfectly true, and we do say it. But you see, good, bad or indifferent, God has appointed *me*. Can you understand a little bit how we walk in the heat of the day today, we the laity? How lost we are! Lost in the brambles and no one to get us out!

Priests try to look like somebody else. In the sixties, they tried to look like the hippies; today, like psychiatrists. Quite a few of them tried to "be chummy" with their flock, trying to be one of the crowd. It doesn't work.

The Russians believe there is great holiness in a sinner. If you've ever read Dostoevsky's *Crime and Punishment,* you remember where the murderer comes to a prostitute. He is astonished to see that she has an Icon with a vigil lamp burning over her bed. He says to her, "Do *you* believe in God?" She answers, "Of course I do!" It is strange, isn't it, that Our Lord canonized the prostitute and the thief? How unimportant is the human quality of a person!

Sure, when I say *your* holiness I mean the holiness of Christ that passes through you because you take a broom and clean that little path for him to walk through. He leaves in your soul a drop of his Precious Blood. Sure, we all want to be holy in the accepted moral sense, but Christ is not a moralist— Christ is God! He doesn't love us because *we* are good; he loves us because *he* is good. We know this very well but we forget it all the time. A Christian believes in the mercy of God. So you can give us mercy because you have the power of that mercy, and our guilty feelings will disappear.

This is the hour for the healing of the Church, and it is you who have to lay your hands upon us, the laity, and on each other, and allow the Holy Spirit to enter. We must forget so many things that the centuries have crammed into our heads and we must return to the Man who was in a hurry and who walked across a little country like Palestine preaching that the kingdom of God is in our midst.

Do the same. Go around preaching it in that strange weakness which is the essence of all holiness. "I glory in my weakness," says St. Paul. But please do it soon, because the Church is in terrible danger from within. The danger is the lack of love of its members for one another.

I implore you, I beg you, as those whom God has left on this earth as an extension of himself. He couldn't leave us alone, you know. He went to his Father and he stayed in you—in the Blessed Sacrament and in you at the Eucharistic Table.

The hour for prayer and fasting is at hand. The healing of the Church, which also means the healing of ourselves, lies in that fasting and that prayer. It will lead us to love. Love will lead us to compassion, and tenderness, and mercy. Like Christ, blown by the wind of the Holy Spirit, you will crisscross the world like a pilgrim. Sitting in your own room wherever you are, or in a monastery or parish, your heart will be wide open to everybody and you will take the whole world in as a shepherd must. You will know that you are a priest to the Hindu, and a priest to the Jew, and a priest to the Christians, and a priest to every human being in this world.

Then the kingdom of Love shall indeed flourish amongst us if you show us how to love one another, how to forgive our enemies, and how to lay down our life for the other. Give us Christ instead of yourself!

The hour is very close, so close. Any day it might explode. True, the Holy Spirit has brought prayer into our midst, and this is quietening the people of God a little. But we still need you, and the Church needs you. You have been ordained for this. You are the Christ in our midst. Help us! Get us out of these brambles! Teach us how to love, how to hope, but above all, help us to renew our faith, for faith is the cradle of both love and hope. There is so little time!

APPENDIX

At the request of the editors, Mrs. Doherty has agreed to append this section of Thomas Merton's *Seven Story Mountain* to her book on the priesthood. It shows in vivid fashion the influence of Mrs. Doherty on the vocation of Thomas Merton, one of the great priests of our time. It is only one instance of many where Mrs. Doherty, through her faith in the priesthood of Jesus Christ, has inspired men to serve the Lord in this sublime calling. We also thought it would be of great interest to our readers to know of the close relationship between these two great lovers of God in our times.

Special thanks to Harcourt, Brace and Company to quote from pp. 357-60 of the book.

The Editors

From the SEVEN STORY MOUNTAIN

by Thomas Merton

"On the third day of the novena, Father Hubert, one of the
Friars, said: 'The Baroness is coming. We are going to drive up
to Buffalo and meet her train from Canada, and bring her
down here. Do you want to come along?' Early in the afternoon
we got in the car, and started north, up one of those long
parallel valleys that slant down towards the Alleghany.

"When the Baroness got off the train, it was the first time I
had seen her with a hat on. But the thing that most impressed
me was the effect she had on these priests. We had been sitting
around in the station, bored, complaining of this and that
situation in the world. Now they were wide awake and cheerful
and listening very attentively to everything she had to say. We
were in a restaurant having something to eat, and the Baroness
was talking about priests, and about the spiritual life and
gratitude, and the ten lepers in the Gospel, of whom only one
returned to give thanks to Christ for having cured them. She
had made what seemed to me to be certainly a good point. But I
suddenly noticed that it had struck the two Friars like a
bombshell.

"Then I realized what was going on. She was preaching to
them. Her visit to St. Bonaventure's was to be, for them and the
Seminarians and the rest who heard her, a kind of a mission, or
a retreat. I had not grasped, before, how much this was part of
her work: priests and religious had become, indirectly, almost
as important a mission field for her as Harlem. It is a
tremendous thing, the economy of the Holy Ghost! When the

Spirit of God finds a soul in which He can work, He uses that soul for any number of purposes: opens out before its eyes a hundred new directions, multiplying its works and its opportunities for the apostolate almost beyond belief and certainly far beyond the ordinary strength of a human being.

"Here was this woman who had started out to conduct a more or less obscure work helping the poor in Harlem, now placed in such a position that the work which had barely been begun was drawing to her souls from every part of the country, and giving her a sort of unofficial apostolate among the priesthood, the clergy and the religious Orders.

"What was it that she had to offer them, that they did not already possess? One thing: she was full of the love of God; and prayer and sacrifice and total, uncompromising poverty had filled her soul with something which, it seemed, these two men had often looked for in vain in the dry and conventional and merely learned retreats that fell to their lot. And I could see that they were drawn to her by the tremendous spiritual vitality of the grace that was in her, a vitality which brought with it a genuine and lasting inspiration, because it put their souls in contact with God as a living reality. And that reality, that contact, is something which we all need: and one of the ways in which it has been decreed that we should arrive at it, is by hearing one another talk about God. *Fides ex auditu.* And it is no novelty for God to raise up saints who are not priests to preach to those who are priests—witness the Baroness's namesake, Catherine of Siena.

"But she had something to say to me, too.

"My turn came when we were in the car, driving south along the shiny wet highway.

"The Baroness was sitting in the front seat, talking to everybody. But presently she turned to me and said:

'Well, Tom, when are you coming to Harlem for good?'

"The simplicity of the question surprised me. Nevertheless, sudden as it was, the idea struck me that this was my answer. This was probably what I had been praying to find out.

"However, it was sudden enough to catch me off my

guard, and I did not quite know what to say. I began to talk about writing. I said that my coming to Harlem depended on how much writing I would be able to do when I got there.

"Both the priests immediately joined in and told me to stop making conditions and opening a lot of loopholds.

'You let her decide about all that,' said Father Hubert.

"So it began to look as if I were going to Harlem, at least for a while.

"The Baroness said: 'Tom, are you thinking of becoming a priest? People who ask all the questions you asked me in those letters usually want to become priests. . . .'

"Her words turned the knife in that old wound. But I said, 'Oh, no, I have no vocation to the priesthood.'

"When the conversation was shifted to something else, I more or less dropped out of it to think over what had been said, and it soon became clear that it was the most plausible thing for me to do. I had no special sense that this was my vocation, but on the other hand I could no longer doubt that St. Bonaventure's had outlived its usefulness in my spiritual life. I did not belong there any more. It was too tame, too safe, too sheltered. It demanded nothing of me. It had no particular cross. It left me to myself, belonging to myself, in full possession of my own will, in full command of all that God had given me that I might give it back to Him. As long as I remained there, I still had given up nothing, or very little, no matter how poor I happened to be.

"At least I could go to Harlem, and join these people in their tenement, and live on what God gave us to eat from day to day, and share my life with the sick and the starving and the dying and those who had never had anything and never would have anything, the outcasts of the earth, a race despised. If that was where I belonged, God would let me know soon enough and definitely enough.

"When we got to St. Bonaventure's, I saw the head of the English Department standing in the dim light under the arched door to the monastery, and I said to the Baroness:

" 'There's my boss. I'll have to go and tell him to hire somebody else for next term if I'm leaving for Harlem.'

"And the next day we made it definite. In January, after the semester was finished, I would come down to live at Friendship House. The Baroness said I would have plenty of time to write in the mornings.

"I went to Father Thomas, the President, in his room in the library, and told him I was going to leave.

"His face became a labyrinth of wrinkles.

" 'Harlem,' he said slowly. 'Harlem.'

"Father Thomas was a man of big silences. There was a long pause before he spoke again: 'Perhaps you are being a bit of an enthusiast.'

"I told him that it seemed to be what I ought to do.

"Another big silence. Then he said: 'Haven't you ever thought of being a priest?'

"Father Thomas was a very wise man, and since he was the head of a seminary and had taught theology to generations of priests, one of the things he might be presumed to know something about was who might or might not have a vocation to the priesthood.

"But I thought: he doesn't know my case. And there was no desire in me to talk about it, to bring up a discussion and get all mixed up now that I had made up my mind to do something definite. So I said:

" 'Oh, yes, I have thought about it, Father. But I don't believe I have that vocation.'

"The words made me unhappy. But I forgot them immediately, when Father Thomas said, with a sigh:

" 'All right, then. Go to Harlem if you must.' "

An Interesting Thought

The publication you have just finished reading is part of the apostolic efforts of the Society of St. Paul of the American Province. A small, unique group of priests and brothers, the members of the Society of St. Paul propose to bring the message of Christ to men through the communications media while living the religious life.

If you know a young man who might be interested in learning more about our life and mission, ask him to contact the Vocation Office in care of the Society of St. Paul, Alba House Community, Canfield, Ohio 44406 (phone 216/533-5503). Full information will be sent without cost or obligation. You may be instrumental in helping a young man to find his vocation in life.
An interesting thought.